SOUTH CAROLINA'S
HISTORIC
RESTAURANTS

and their recipes

SOUTH
CAROLINA'S

JOHN F. BLAIR, *Publisher*
Winston-Salem, North Carolina

HISTORIC RESTAURANTS

and their recipes

**by DAWN O'BRIEN
and KAREN MULFORD**

Drawings by Bob Anderson

Library of Congress Cataloging in Publication Data

O'Brien, Dawn.
South Carolina's historic restaurants and their recipes.

Includes index.
1. Cookery, American—Southern style.   2. Cookery—
South Carolina.   3. Restaurants, lunch rooms, etc.—
South Carolina.   4. Historic buildings—South Carolina.
I. Mulford, Karen.   II. Title.
TX715.0'287   1984   641.5'09757   84-18556
ISBN 0-89587-041-X

DEDICATION

I believe the most important gift a child can receive is a sense of self-worth. Both of my late grandmothers, Etta Lee and Goldie West, knew how to inspire this feeling. Therefore, even though neither is alive to see how their gift is manifesting itself, I dedicate this book to them.

Dawn O'Brien

I'd like to thank my husband, Jon, and my sons, Sean and Justin, for their remarkable patience during the months of travel, research and writing involved in this book. Special thanks go to my parents, Bill and Leona Surina, for their encouraging support of this project—and all the others I've undertaken during my life.

Karen Mulford

ACKNOWLEDGMENTS

A project of this scope is a collaborative labor involving more people than just the writers. For those individuals and agencies who gave us help through endorsement, encouragement or the sharing of special skills, we are thankful.

To: The chefs who shared their secrets with us—especially those who, due to language barriers, took us back to their kitchens and taught us, step-by-step, their unique methods of preparation.

To: The restaurateurs who helped us discover the rich heritage of their establishments.

To: The artist, Bob Anderson, whose talent and persistent interest in our project resulted in the magnificent pen and ink renderings of the restaurants.

To: South Carolina's Division of Tourism, especially Director Robert G. Liming, travel writer Waltene G. Vaughn, Alice T. Hite, Joanna Angle, Jayne T. Redman, Diane Raef and Kevin Crown.

To: The many branches of South Carolina's Chamber of Commerce that provided material and assistance.

To: Betty Jo Gilley, Leona Surina and Irma and Bill Joyce, who helped us test and retest recipes in the areas of their culinary expertise.

To: John, Shannon Heather and Daintry O'Brien for their continuing patience and interest in developing more sophisticated palates.

To: All our guinea pigs who ate the testing dishes, particularly those who gave us confidence when they asked for second helpings.

FOREWORD From a contemporary sage comes this wisdom: "You can never be too rich or too thin." Neither condition has ever plagued me. But, after feasting my way through North Carolina's and Virginia's historic restaurants, it became clear that, travel- and time-wise, I *could* spread myself too thin. I needed a collaborator to share the "oh so tough grind" of dining lavishly. After interviewing a herd of hungry writers, I met Karen Mulford, and we clicked instantly. Maybe it's because we are both transplanted Westerners; I can't explain it. But in spite of living for many years below the Mason-Dixon line, neither of us has lost our appreciation for things Southern.

Even with such instant rapport, we privately wondered if one of us would end up killing the other. (Harsher thoughts have occurred to collaborators.) Instead, it has been a very positive experience. Karen feels that it has been a great apprenticeship, while I have gained through a reinforcement of my impressions and ideas. And, yes, frustrations—even the tiny ones—are more bearable when they are shared. For instance, Karen's son Sean, after sinking his teeth into The Chart House's Mud Pie, became indignant: "You mean we only get to eat this once?"

Because the sharing of my restaurant experience has always been with my readers, it was particularly fun for me to see Karen race into Philippe Million Restaurant to meet me one evening. We had decided earlier that day to divide the appointments, and she could have gone to our inn and taken a nap, but the excitement this restaurant promised was too much of a temptation for her to miss.

Throughout our joint and separate travels we found that a specific question continually surfaced: "Is this building historic, or is it just old?" The answer lies in the definition of history and is one that is argued with unresolved scholarly pursuit.

Some historians believe a structure should be considered historic only if a significant national or regional event has occurred there. This view, in our opinion, denies the contri-

ix

butions of many of our nation's people. We feel that everyday people played a major role in the formation of our country's values. True, famed statesmen contributed to our lawmaking process, and their names are recorded in our textbooks, as they should be. Unrecorded, though, are those who helped to build our country through their simple daily toil. We think they count equally. Therefore, we have chosen not to ignore a beautiful old church, warehouse, ice house or post office simply because it was not the site of an event significant enough to be included in our history books.

Age is, of course, a basic factor in the formulation of historical criteria. Any structure less than fifty years old does not qualify. In researching the historic structures that have been transformed into restaurants in South Carolina, we have conformed to this requirement, with one exception: Rice Planters Restaurant in Myrtle Beach. This building was constructed from over-one-hundred-year-old materials, and we feel this tie to the past makes the restaurant a worthy candidate. After all, one of the criteria we value most is the preservation of materials that otherwise would have been destroyed.

We believe dining should be an event, not just a habit. In essence, this means that the atmosphere must equal the food. Thus, just as in the books on North Carolina's and Virginia's historic restaurants, not every historic restaurant in South Carolina is included in this book. Within the framework of our criteria, which is as subjective as it is objective, not all the historic restaurants we visited meet the standards that contribute to an enjoyable dining experience. Also, there are a few restaurants that are not included because they were not interested in participating or did not want to share their histories or recipes with us.

Incidentally, we feel it is important for readers to know that every recipe has been tested and, in some instances, modified for home use. My daughter Heather, now a recipe-testing veteran, often is asked which dish is her favorite. Recently I overheard her answer: "Which category? If we're talking entrées, it was that raspberry sauce on top of veal" (The Wine Cellar's Veal Medallions with Raspberry Sauce). "But with vegetables, now that would be those wonderful, huge baked potatoes with everything imaginable stuffed in them" (Molly Morgan's Stuffed Potatoes). My husband John interrupted any further recitations with, "What about The Parson's Table's Chicken Oskar, and oh, yeah, the Very Very Carrots from Greylogs?" This enthusiasm should encourage readers to try even the seemingly difficult recipes. Believe me, it's not impossible to achieve fabulous results in your own kitchen.

Karen relates that her husband Jon favored the seafood dishes and Hartzog's Tea Room's Applesauce Muffins, a choice our editor, Noël Todd-McLaughlin, seconds. This is one of the perks of being a food editor; you get the second shot at trying out what makes you hungry.

From the experiences and feedback we have encountered in testing and serving these recipes, it can only be said that feasts await you, whether in South Carolina's historic restaurants or in your own kitchen. Bon Appétit!

CONTENTS

State of South Carolina

Office of the Governor

RICHARD W. RILEY
GOVERNOR

POST OFFICE BOX 11450
COLUMBIA 29211

South Carolina, eighth of the original thirteen colonies, has painstakingly blended the best of a gracious past with the proud achievements of today. With a rich history that reaches back 4,000 years to the first indications of Indian settlements, the Palmetto State has witnessed the rapid growth of the colonial period, the shattering effects and aftermath of the Civil War, and the birth of a strong and new economy as part of the New South.

The preparation of food and dining in South Carolina has played a very important role in the state's history. In this book, Dawn O'Brien and Karen Mulford have provided a different perspective on various South Carolina restaurants, which are storehouses of historic lore and charm.

Although not an exhaustive listing, the 50 restaurants described on the following pages represent the diversity of the state itself. Beginning in Charleston, where the first English settlement occurred more than 300 years ago, the authors feature several of the state's quaint restaurants specializing in succulent Low Country cuisine. This excursion continues toward the Midlands, which is dominated by Columbia, the state's capital. The trip ends in the state's Up Country, where mouthwatering dishes are just as superb as the area's majestic scenery.

I hope that you will enjoy reading the descriptions of the restaurants and even try some of the recipes found in the book. Furthermore, I hope that the reading will entice you to visit beautiful South Carolina and sample some of the delicious dishes handsomely served in these historic buildings.

Richard W. Riley

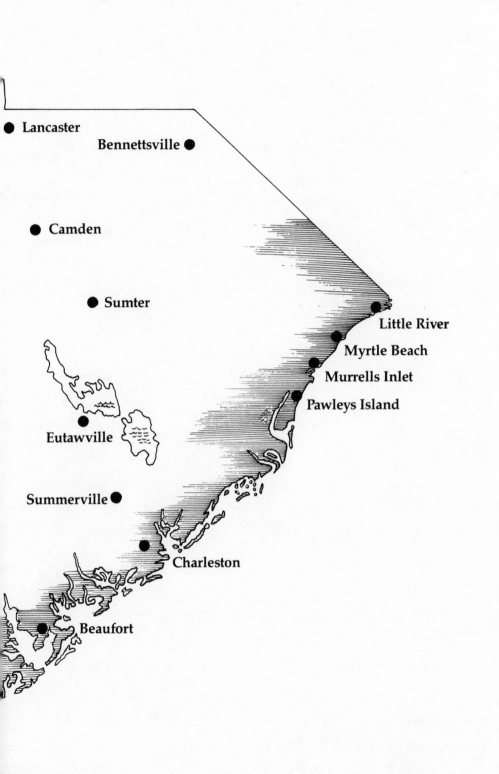

Lancaster

Bennettsville

Camden

Sumter

Little River

Myrtle Beach

Murrells Inlet

Pawleys Island

Eutawville

Summerville

Charleston

Beaufort

THE PARSON'S TABLE
RESTAURANT
Little River

THE PARSON'S TABLE

Did you ever buy a clothing accessory so fantastic that you assembled an entire outfit around it? Then you will understand what restaurateur Toby Frye did. He rescued some magnificent opalescent stained-glass windows, which meant that he needed to find an equally magnificent location for their display. Since the stained glass was salvaged from churches, what could be more suitable than the Little River Methodist Church?

Frye had the 1885 weathered pine church moved to its present location, and then he set about the business of designing one of the most sophisticated interiors I've ever seen. Until the sign above the entrance is read, you just think you've stumbled upon a meticulously kept old church. The picket fence and gazebo suggest an earlier period, a time when this part of the beach area was a little sailing village. Since the area was poor, the little church had no stained-glass windows until Frye decided to turn it into a restaurant.

The interior reminded me a bit of Maxwell Plum's in New York. Some of the stained glass is lighted from the back and used to artistically partition the dining room and the kitchen. In one room the stained glass forms the ceiling. The jeweled splendor of the glass renders such a magnificent effect that you wonder if the cuisine will be anticlimactic. It is not.

Participating in a contest of sorts, I alternately sipped a very expensive wine and The Parson's Table's house wine. Yes, there was a difference, but not an especially appreciable one. Their wine list is as scrupulously selected as their entrées. My dinner was so scrumptiously orchestrated that I wondered how I would ever be able to duplicate it in my own kitchen.

My worries about testing these recipes at home were groundless. I tried both their Chicken Oskar and their Coquille Saint Jacques. Each is distinct in taste, but the preparation is similar. The light breading of the sautéed scallops makes that dish, encased in a delicate crust, particularly juicy. The Chicken Oskar is a new variation of a dish usually made with veal, and it's very easy on the palate.

Two of their steak entrées, named Cathedral and Chapel,

are the only references to the building's original use. I'm glad they refrained from such cute appellations as "hedonistic" and "sinful" to describe their desserts—even if they are.

Their Amaretto Cheesecake with Barclay Sauce is the kind of mirage I'd see if stranded in the desert. It's so rich that a sliver is all you can manage, but it's a recipe that will make you famous. That's exactly what chef Bill Moelich's continental cuisine has done for this stunning restaurant.

The Parson's Table Restaurant is located 6 miles north of North Myrtle Beach in Little River off Highway 17. Dinner is served from 5:30 p.m. until 10:00 p.m., Monday through Saturday. The restaurant is open March 1 through December 15. For reservations (preferred) call (803) 249–3702.

THE PARSON'S TABLE RESTAURANT'S
CHICKEN OSKAR

4 boneless chicken breasts
1 cup flour
1 teaspoon salt
½ teaspoon pepper
½ teaspoon paprika
2 to 3 eggs, beaten
pinch of basil
1 cup Japanese or Italian
   bread crumbs

4 tablespoons butter
2 tablespoons oil
8 asparagus spears, canned
   (or fresh asparagus,
   steamed)
6 ounces backfin crabmeat
hollandaise sauce
   (commercial or
   homemade)

Flatten the chicken with a mallet on both sides. Dredge the chicken in flour seasoned with salt, pepper and paprika. Dip chicken in eggs. Mix basil into the bread crumbs and roll chicken in the mixture. In a large skillet, heat 2 tablespoons of the butter and all the oil. Sauté chicken until lightly browned. Remove and keep in warm oven. Heat asparagus and crabmeat in remaining butter over low heat until heated through. Put chicken on oven-proof plates and top with crabmeat and asparagus. Spoon hollandaise over top of each portion and place under broiler until light brown. Serves 4.

3

THE PARSON'S TABLE RESTAURANT'S AMARETTO CHEESECAKE WITH BARCLAY SAUCE

1 Graham Cracker Crust (see Index)	½ cup whipping cream
	1 teaspoon salt
2½ pounds of cream cheese	1 tablespoon almond extract
1½ cups sugar	3 ounces amaretto
1 packet unflavored gelatin	5 eggs

Prepare Graham Cracker Crust, and press it into a greased, 10-inch springform pan and bake. Allow cream cheese to reach room temperature and cut into chunks. With an electric mixer, alternately combine cream cheese with sugar, and blend for 15 to 20 minutes. Dissolve gelatin in whipping cream over low heat, whisking constantly. Add to cream cheese mixture when gelatin is dissolved. Add remaining ingredients, and mix on low speed until well combined. Pour batter into the crust, and set the springform pan into a large roasting pan placed on your oven rack. Pour water around the springform pan, being careful not to spill any water into batter. Water should cover two-thirds the height of the cake pan. Bake at 300 degrees for about 2 hours, or until a toothpick comes out clean when inserted into cake. Let cake cool and refrigerate several hours. Yields 1 cake.

Barclay Sauce:

1 10-ounce package frozen strawberries or raspberries (or 5 ounces of each)	1 cup creme de cassis or dry white wine
	1 shaved square unsweetened chocolate
1 10-ounce jar strawberry preserves	

Place berries, preserves and creme de cassis (or wine) in a blender, and puree until smooth. Cut Cheesecake and pour sauce over each slice. Garnish with shaved chocolate. Yields 3½ cups.

4

RICE PLANTERS RESTAURANT
Myrtle Beach

**RICE PLANTERS
RESTAURANT**

There's not a doubt in my mind that George Washington would have dined at Rice Planters if the restaurant had been here when he rode through in 1791. Washington was a renowned connoisseur of fine food, and it is said that he didn't mind traveling a little farther to those restaurants that exerted special skills in the culinary department.

Part of the purpose for Washington's journey to the Low Country was to study successful rice planting techniques. Rice, as an agricultural crop, made its debut in the 1680s when a ship out of Madagascar put into port at Charleston for repairs. The ship's cargo was rice, and the story goes that a peck of the grain, complete with instructions for cultivation, was sold to a local plantation owner. That rice crop produced a longer and more flavorful grain than did the typical Chinese rice, and it introduced Low Country planters to an agricultural product that helped to build great fortunes.

Rice planters became the pacesetters of their day, building and decorating magnificent plantation homes with the finest English furnishings. It became the style to import European craftsmen for the construction of the manor houses. In fact, so close was the tie to England that rice planters were among the last to side with the colonists.

Most of the structural material at Rice Planters Restaurant was salvaged from area rice plantations and coastal warehouses. The salt-treated walls in the downstairs of the restaurant came from a Charleston warehouse. Every time the weather changes, the walls turn a different color.

My favorite place to dine at Rice Planters is the upstairs dining room that juts out over a serene creek. A frozen Daiquiri turned out to be the right accompaniment for their complimentary Pepper Cheese Spread, which became addictive.

She-crab Soup is a premium item here, but my real love was the Mariner's Shrimp Creole Casserole, served with a green salad and a loaf of fresh baked bread. Another good selection is their sautéed Onions and Chicken Livers. All true

6

Southerners and converts will enjoy the old-fashioned Pecan Pie for dessert.

Be sure to take a tour of the facility. The restaurant pays homage to the rice planters with historical artifacts displayed in every room.

Rice Planters Restaurant is located at 6707 Kings Highway North in Myrtle Beach. Dinner is served daily from 5:00 p.m. until 10:00 p.m. Reservations are not accepted. The phone number is (803) 449–3456.

RICE PLANTERS RESTAURANT'S SHE-CRAB SOUP

1 stick margarine
2 tablespoons chicken base
¾ cup self-rising flour
2 5⅓-ounce cans evaporated milk
1 quart water
2 tablespoons grated onions
1 hard-boiled egg, diced
¼ to ½ teaspoon monosodium glutamate or salt
¾ teaspoon black pepper
½ pound claw crabmeat
¼ to ½ teaspoon mace
sherry (1 teaspoon per bowl)

In the top of a double boiler, place margarine, chicken base and flour, and mix to form a smooth paste. Place paste in large pot or Dutch oven and add all remaining ingredients except sherry. Cook over medium heat, about 45 minutes to 1 hour, stirring frequently. More water may be added if mixture becomes too thick. Serve hot with a teaspoon of sherry added to each bowl. Yields 2 quarts.

RICE PLANTERS RESTAURANT'S PEPPER CHEESE SPREAD

1 pound sharp Cheddar cheese
4 tablespoons plus 1 teaspoon corn oil
¾ teaspoon red pepper flakes
¾ teaspoon cayenne pepper
3 tablespoons plus 1 teaspoon finely chopped banana peppers

7

Set out cheese until it reaches room temperature and cut into small cubes. By hand, combine the cheese with oil, red pepper flakes, cayenne pepper and banana peppers. Do not use an electric mixer. Refrigerate. Serve with saltines or melba toast. Yields 1½ cups.

RICE PLANTERS RESTAURANT'S
MARINER'S SHRIMP CREOLE CASSEROLE

1 pound medium shrimp,
  peeled and deveined
2 tablespoons oil or butter
¼ cup chopped bell
  peppers
1 cup chopped onions
3 celery ribs, thinly sliced
1 garlic clove, chopped
3 tablespoons flour
1 teaspoon salt
2 teaspoons chili powder
1 teaspoon pepper

2 tablespoons sugar
¼ teaspoon sage
¼ teaspoon thyme
¼ cup green olives
½ cup canned tomatoes,
  mashed
1 cup canned small peas
1 cup chopped fresh
  mushrooms
1 cup water
rice (follow package
  directions)

Cook shrimp in boiling water for about 2 minutes; remove and set aside. Place oil in a skillet and sauté bell peppers, onions, celery and garlic. Place sautéed mixture in a large pot or Dutch oven. Add all remaining ingredients except shrimp and rice; cook on low heat for 45 minutes to 1 hour. Combine shrimp with sauce, and serve over cooked rice. Serves 4.

OLIVER'S LODGE DINING ROOM
Murrells Inlet

**OLIVER'S LODGE
DINING ROOM**

I knew that a reference to "the real McCoy" meant that something wasn't an imitation, but I didn't realize its true significance until I lunched at Oliver's Lodge Dining Room. The actual McCoy brothers not only lunched here but also stayed in this waterfront lodge during their rum-running days. It was their pure, undiluted whiskey that earned the brothers a reputation for honesty. The government, however, had a different definition of honesty and sent the lawbreakers to prison. Ironically, the McCoys' internment provided Oliver's with artistic dividends.

A grouping of unusually fine seascapes, which the brothers painted while serving time in prison, now hangs in the restaurant. A perfectly rendered replica of their ship was painted on a brown paper bag, a canvas which deserves a mark for resourcefulness. As I admired the McCoys' skill, a typical Low Country meal of delicious Hush Puppies, Green Salad (with Oliver's own tangy Oil and Vinegar Dressing) and tasty Mushroom Shrimp Creole was set before me on a wooden table. The eighty-year-old table was built by Captain Mac Oliver, the lodge's first owner, who was pretty resourceful himself.

But then Oliver's has always been a testament to Low Country ingenuity. This sturdy heart pine house was built sometime after 1860. Although current owner Maxine Oliver Hawkins says "it looks as if it's going to fall down," it isn't. Oliver's is merely authentic rusticity. As Mr. Hawkins jokes, "It's the only place I know of that a coat of paint would ruin."

The interior has retained a homey atmosphere that you just don't run across in newer establishments. The collection of china and porcelain cheese keepers that belonged to Grandmother Emma Oliver is attractively arranged on antique sideboards. Little touches like these, and the tasty fresh fish and Corn Dodgers, keep customers coming back.

The day that I was at Oliver's, a woman who was dining with her grandchildren stopped by and shared with me her childhood memories of visiting this old landmark. Apparently, good memories keep her coming back year after year. Another customer is the famed mystery writer, Mickey Spillane, the restaurant's friend for over twenty-five years. Spillane chose this old lodge as the place where he and his bride were married.

Oliver's Lodge Dining Room is located off Highway 17 next to Belin Methodist Church in Murrells Inlet. Dinner is served from 4:00 p.m. until 10:00 p.m., Monday through Saturday. The restaurant is open from March 15 until Thanksgiving. Reservations are not accepted, but the phone number is (803) 651–2963.

OLIVER'S LODGE DINING ROOM'S
CORN DODGERS

1 cup yellow cornmeal	2 eggs, well beaten
¾ cup self-rising flour	1 cup milk
½ teaspoon baking powder	2 tablespoons vegetable oil
½ teaspoon salt	fat for deep frying
2 tablespoons sugar	

Mix first 5 ingredients in a bowl, blending well. Add eggs, milk and oil and beat mixture well. Heat fat to 350 degrees. With your fingers, push about a ½ tablespoon of dough from the spoon into deep fat, repeating until all the dough is used up. Take the spoon and roll the mixture over when it pops to the surface in order to brown evenly. Remove when golden brown, usually within a minute. Place on paper towel to drain. Keep warm before serving. Serves 6 to 8.

OLIVER'S LODGE DINING ROOM'S
OIL AND VINEGAR DRESSING

½ cup cider vinegar	½ tablespoon garlic powder
1 cup vegetable oil	½ tablespoon
½ tablespoon Tabasco sauce	Worcestershire sauce

11

Place all ingredients in a jar or blender, and mix well until thoroughly blended. Refrigerate. Shake jar before serving. Yields 1½ cups.

OLIVER'S LODGE DINING ROOM'S
MUSHROOM SHRIMP CREOLE

6 slices bacon
3 ribs thinly sliced celery
1½ large onions, chopped
1 bell pepper, chopped
1 16-ounce can tomatoes,
   mashed with juice
½ teaspoon thyme
1½ teaspoons oregano
dash of commercial hot
   sauce
salt and pepper to taste
6 large, fresh mushrooms,
   sliced
2 pounds shrimp, boiled
2 cups cooked rice (follow
   package directions)

In a large skillet, fry bacon until crisp. Remove it from the skillet and crumble. Sauté celery, onions and pepper in bacon grease until tender. Add mashed tomatoes with juice and crumbled bacon. Stir in thyme, oregano, hot sauce, salt and pepper. Cook one hour on low heat, stirring often. Add mushrooms and cook for an additional 30 minutes. Add cooked shrimp to the sauce when ready to serve. Spoon creole over rice. Serves 4 to 5.

NOTE: Sauce and shrimp may be frozen, but they must be kept in separate containers.

PLANTERS BACK PORCH
RESTAURANT
Murrells Inlet

PLANTERS BACK PORCH RESTAURANT

An accident, rather than necessity, often mothers invention. At least that was the case when an accident occurred many years ago in a turpentine plant. It seems that a worker mistakenly dropped a raw potato into an iron vat of bubbling hot pine rosin. The potato sank out of sight, but some twenty minutes later it reappeared on the surface of the heavy rosin. The worker scooped the potato out of the rosin and ate it, reporting that it was the best he'd ever tasted. Word of his discovery spread throughout the pine belt of the South. In no time, almost all the plantations in the area had their own pots for cooking the "rosin taters."

A big rosin vat is exactly what I found in the kitchen at Planters Back Porch Restaurant. I was a bit skeptical until I sampled this tasty potato. After one bite, I began trying to figure just where a rosin vat could be installed in my kitchen. Space immediately ruled out the idea, so I'll just have to be content with the pleasant thought of returning to this lovely Low Country farmhouse.

The house was built in 1887 by the Eason family, who grew tobacco, cotton and corn. The only planting done today occurs in the flower garden, ensuring that something lovely blooms throughout the year. The garden motif was chosen for the restaurant because, in the 1880s, entertaining was done on the wide back porches that connected the Low Country houses with the gardens and summer kitchens in the back. Century-old pecan trees still shade this porch, and the original smokehouse remains in the garden, but it has since been attached to the main house.

The bar overlooks the garden, and that is where I first was introduced to a drink called Inlet Sunset. It's a kind of thick orange piña colada that reminds me of the frozen orange popsicles we used to buy from the ice cream man, although it definitely delivers more of a punch. The logia-styled bar is decorated to reflect a garden setting, as are all the dining rooms. Grassy green tones underline a bevy of rich, parrot colors. These brilliant hues are set off by white lattice work.

Along with a dry, light bottle of Chenin Blanc Sebastiani 1982, I chose the Panned Seafood Variety for dinner. This entrée is served in individual cast-iron skillets and contains lobster, lump crabmeat and shrimp in a buttery sauce. I never get enough of fresh seafood, so my dinner companions shared a yummy bite of Crabmeat au Gratin with me, and I allowed them a taste of the rosin-baked potato. With this potato you can avoid extra calories, because it's delicious without butter or sour cream. With broiled fish, a green salad and a slice of watermelon, your waistline won't suffer.

If you'd rather think about counting calories tomorrow, then I heartily suggest their Black Bottom Dessert Drink. This is a recipe you can whip up quickly. Then, while sitting on your porch, the entire adventure of dining at this charming old restaurant can be relived.

Planters Back Porch Restaurant is located on the corner of Highway 17 South and Wachesaw Road in Murrells Inlet. Dinner is served from 4:30 p.m. until 10:00 p.m., daily. The restaurant is open February 15 through December 1. Reservations are not accepted. The phone numbers are (803) 651–5263 and 651–5544.

PLANTERS BACK PORCH RESTAURANT'S
BLACK BOTTOM DESSERT DRINK

1 quart chocolate ice cream
4 ounces Kahlúa
whipped cream

1 square bittersweet
   chocolate
4 maraschino cherries
4 straws

Fill blender within an inch of the top with loosely packed ice cream. Add Kahlúa. Turn blender on and off quickly to remove lumps from ice cream, but do not blend until smooth. Spoon into four 16-ounce bubble glasses. Top with desired amount of whipped cream, and grate chocolate over top. Add cherries and a straw to each glass. Serves 4.

PLANTERS BACK PORCH RESTAURANT'S
INLET SUNSET

4 ounces crushed ice
2 teaspoons commercial
  liquid piña colada mix
2 generous scoops orange
  sherbet
1 ounce Orgeat's syrup

3 ounces commercial
  powdered sour mix
1½ ounces vodka
whipped cream
1 maraschino cherry

Place crushed ice, piña colada mix, orange sherbet, Oregeat's syrup, sour mix and vodka in a blender container. Blend until frothy and pour into a large glass. Top with desired amount of whipped cream and a maraschino cherry. Serves 1.

PLANTERS BACK PORCH RESTAURANT'S
PANNED SEAFOOD VARIETY

½ pound small shrimp,
  cleaned and deveined
1 pound Alaskan king
  crabmeat
2 pounds white backfin
  crabmeat

4 to 5 tablespoons cubed
  butter
dash paprika
fresh parsley sprigs for
  garnish

In boiling water, cook shrimp for 2 minutes. Drain the shrimp and let it cool. Chop crabmeat into small lumps. Combine shrimp and crabmeat, mixing thoroughly. Grease a large cast-iron skillet or baking dish and spread mixture evenly over bottom. Dot with cubed butter. Place in a 300-degree oven for 8 to 10 minutes. Place under broiler for 1 minute. Stir to mix butter through mixture before serving. Sprinkle with paprika and garnish with parsley. Serves 8 to 10.

NOTE: This dish also can be prepared using chopped lobster instead of, or in addition to, shrimp.

CASSENA INN
Pawleys Island

CASSENA INN

Pawleys Island offers a quiet, noncommercial sanctuary for the world's weary that has been attracting visitors since the 1700s. Plantation families sought refuge on the island then to escape the dreaded malaria-carrying mosquitos, which wouldn't cross the salt marsh between Pawleys Island and the mainland. Although we're no longer fleeing mosquitos, the island continues to offer seclusion for those of us who seek escape of a different nature.

Bumper stickers boast that Pawleys Island is "arrogantly shabby," but that was not what I witnessed in the Cassena Inn's 1917 dining room. True, there are no crystal chandeliers, oriental carpets or Queen Anne chairs. In fact, the dining room has a simple, almost Puritan-like atmosphere. The spartan furnishings are ameliorated, however, by some cheerful touches. For instance, on the morning I breakfasted at the inn, wildflowers cascaded from the lovely antique pitcher situated across from my table.

Breakfast isn't a big number with me, but who can resist freshly squeezed orange juice, made-from-scratch Pecan Bread, Scrambled Eggs, Sausage, French Toast prepared with homemade French bread, Hash Brown Potatoes and Cheese Grits? Had I known those Grits were going to be so good, I would have tried to pry the recipe from the chef.

During the warmer months, evening guests dine on the inn's screened wraparound porch, where they practically are swathed in jungle-like vegetation. Dinner entrées include such Low Country offerings as Stuffed Flounder, Smoked Pork Loin with Glazed Apricots, Oyster Pie and freshly baked cobblers and pies. The wine and beer list, like the menu, varies with the seasons, but you always may be assured of a tasty selection.

The chef made a face when I asked about dieters, since people usually come to Pawleys Island to let go, not diet. Nevertheless, the inn will scare up some broiled fish, shrimp or a chef salad if you want to, or need to, maintain a special diet.

Cassena Inn is located off Highway 17 on Pawleys Island. The inn is open May 23 through October 31. Breakfast is served at 8:30 a.m. Dinner is served at 7:30 p.m. There is only one seating for each meal, and reservations are required. Call (803) 237–2666.

CASSENA INN'S SMOKED PORK LOIN WITH GLAZED APRICOTS

5-pound smoked pork loin
¼ cup salad oil
2 carrots, sliced
2 celery stalks, sliced
¼ teaspoon sage
1 bay leaf
1 tablespoon salt
¾ teaspoon pepper

1 cup white wine
2 cups brown sauce (commercial or homemade)
1 quart boiling water
¾ pound dried apricots
¾ cup unfiltered honey

Place pork in roasting pan with oil. Roast at 400 degrees for 15 minutes; remove. Combine carrots, celery, sage, bay leaf, salt, pepper, wine and brown sauce. Pour over pork. Cover and roast at 300 degrees for approximately 1 hour and 15 minutes, basting 2 to 3 times. Meanwhile, pour boiling water over apricots. Let stand 20 minutes and drain well. Combine apricots and honey in saucepan and simmer 10 minutes. Pour apricot-honey glaze over sliced pork loin just before serving. Serves 10 to 12.

CASSENA INN'S TANGERINE YAMS

2 pounds fresh, medium-sized yams

3 tangerines
¾ cup unfiltered honey

Cook unpeeled yams in boiling water. Peel and slice yams lengthwise into quarters and arrange in a greased baking pan. Place peeled tangerine sections on yams. Pour honey over yams and tangerines, and bake at 375 degrees for 15 to 18 minutes. Serves 6.

CASSENA INN'S PECAN BREAD

2½ cups sifted, all-purpose
flour
1 cup sugar
1 teaspoon salt

2 teaspoons baking powder
2 cups chopped pecans
2 eggs
1 cup half and half

Sift flour, sugar, salt and baking powder together in a mixing bowl and stir in the pecans. Mix until blended. Beat eggs in a separate bowl until foamy. Add half and half to eggs, and stir into the flour-nut mixture. Pour into a greased loaf pan and bake in a preheated oven at 350 degrees for one hour. Turn out of pan onto rack and cool. Yields 1 loaf.

CASSENA INN'S OYSTER SAUCE

2 tablespoons butter
2 tablespoons flour
1 cup milk
1 tablespoon Worcestershire
sauce

salt and pepper to taste
3 tablespoons finely
chopped fresh parsley
1 cup finely chopped oysters
oyster liquid

Melt butter in a skillet and stir in flour to make a roux. Add milk and stir until smooth. Season with Worcestershire sauce, salt and pepper. Heat to a boil. Stir in parsley, oysters and oyster liquid and heat through. Excellent with turkey and broiled seafood. Yields 2 cups.

THE PAWLEYS ISLAND INN
RESTAURANT AND BAKERY
Pawleys Island

PAWLEYS ISLAND
INN

Eclectic clutter could describe my office décor these days. For instance, an imprint from an original postal marking stamp hangs from my blackboard, reminding me of The Pawleys Island Inn Bakery. Needing goodies to take home, I flew into this highly recommended bakery and found people having lunch in the hundred-year-old building that once served as the post office on the Waverly plantation. The paper that now adorns my blackboard came from one of the packages I bought there. It was imprinted with the old plantation's postal stamp.

During the plantation's heyday, the mail was transported neither by stagecoach nor train. Instead, both the rice cargo and mail were delivered via the Waccamaw River. I learned that the plantation's rice mills were once on par with the largest in South Carolina. The plantation was such a vast enterprise that it had its own post office.

Since I was meeting friends for lunch next door at Pawleys Island Inn Restaurant and Bar, I decided to sample only a few of the offerings in this tiny bakery, where I was intoxicated with the aroma of fresh bread and pastries.

Sitting at an ice cream parlor table, I sipped their homemade He-crab Soup while nibbling on a wondrous Duckling Terrine in a Buttermilk Scone. I had stopped only for their Swiss Almond Slice, but I couldn't leave without adding Mount Blancs, Linzer Tarts, Petit Fours and Buttermilk Scones.

A blackboard told me that I could have ordered Shrimp Salad, a quiche or a sandwich made with their homemade bread. A bakery is not a place for counting calories, but you *can* diet next door at The Pawleys Island Inn Restaurant and Bar.

This restaurant has been reconstructed, using some old materials from Waverly, in the mode of an original Low Country plantation home. Due to the high water table, the lower floor cellar was built of brick for wine cooling and food storage, while the upper floors were used as living quarters.

I dined with my friends on the ground level dining room

just beyond the bar. Arriving a tad late from my bakery adventure, I heard my friends singing the praises of a Grand Cru. This wine was a Graves, Chateau Carbonnieux. While they ordered Grilled Fish from the restaurant's famous mesquite grill, I followed the suggestion of the restaurateur, who steered me in the direction of a light but luscious Pasta Primavera, which raced to the top of my recipe list.

I didn't leave Pawleys Island empty handed. On the contrary, I drove home with boxes of pastries, crawfish on ice, the inevitable Pawleys Island hammock and the postmarked paper from my confectionary discovery.

The Pawleys Island Inn Bakery and The Pawleys Island Inn Restaurant and Bar are located in the Hammock Shop Plantation Stores off Highway 17 in Pawleys Island. Lunch is served at the bakery from 10:00 a.m. until 5:00 p.m., Monday through Saturday. The telephone number is (803) 237–4809. Lunch is served at the restaurant from 11:00 a.m. until 3:00 p.m., and dinner is served from 6:00 p.m. until 10:00 p.m., Monday through Saturday. For reservations (recommended for dinner) call (803) 237–8491.

THE PAWLEYS ISLAND INN RESTAURANT'S PASTA PRIMAVERA

1½ sticks butter
1 cup grated Romano cheese
1 cup heavy cream
1 medium red bell pepper, seeded and julienned
1 tomato, peeled and diced
2 garlic cloves, minced
1 teaspoon fresh basil leaves, diced
3 tablespoons olive oil
3 tablespoons pine nuts

½ cup fresh mushrooms, quartered
½ cup diced eggplant
¼ cup broccoli florets, blanched
¼ cup cauliflower, blanched
¼ cup snow peas, blanched
1 pound fettuccine, cooked
¼ cup coarsely chopped fresh parsley

Melt 1 stick of butter with the cheese and heavy cream over medium-high heat, whipping constantly until sauce becomes smooth. Set aside. Melt remaining butter in a skillet, and sauté pepper, tomato, garlic and basil until tender. In a separate pan, add olive oil and sauté pine nuts, mushrooms and eggplant until lightly browned. Add broccoli, cauliflower, red pepper mixture and cheese sauce. Heat until bubbly, then add snow peas and fettuccine, allowing mixture to heat through as it is tossed. Turn onto platter and garnish with parsley. Serves 4.

THE PAWLEYS ISLAND INN BAKERY'S IRISH SODA BREAD WITH RAISINS

1 cup of cake flour
1 cup whole wheat flour
½ teaspoon baking powder
1 teaspoon salt
½ cup brown sugar
1 teaspoon cinnamon

2 tablespoons butter, cubed
½ teaspoon baking soda
1 cup buttermilk
1 egg, beaten
½ cup raisins

Salt Water Wash:
1 cup water   2 teaspoons salt

In a large mixing bowl, sift together all the dry ingredients except the baking soda. Rub butter in with fingertips until absorbed into mixture. Dissolve the baking soda in buttermilk, and stir until well mixed. Add buttermilk mixture to dry mixture, stirring lightly until combined. Add the egg and mix only until thoroughly incorporated. Add raisins. Knead for a few minutes, but do not overwork the dough. Grease a baking sheet and place dough on the sheet, shaping until it is round. Flatten slightly. Wash with salt water mixture, then dust heavily with flour. Cut a large X about one-half inch deep on top. Bake in a preheated 375-degree oven for approximately 20 minutes. Bread should sound hollow when tapped lightly on the bottom. Yields 1 loaf.

82 QUEEN
Charleston

82 QUEEN In Charleston, the best antidote for depression is a trip to 82 Queen. We had driven through a four-hour rainstorm the day we visited, and our enthusiasm was damp. But our spirits began to lift as soon as we opened the wrought iron gate and threaded our way through the century-old courtyard into the covered patio dining area. The serenity of a private garden can lend a tranquilizing touch to most anyone's mood. And lunching opposite the arched windows secured from author Margaret Mitchell's estate added an interesting note.

After a few minutes on the plant-filled patio, Karen and I were revitalized and very hungry. The first thing we discovered was the She-crab Soup, richly spiced with sizable chunks of crabmeat. Every coastal restaurant seems to have its own special recipe for this soup, but 82 Queen's sherry-flavored She-crab is one of the best we've ever tasted.

When our salads arrived, my first impression was that they were too pretty to eat. The 82 House Salad is a collage of Romaine lettuce, mushrooms, red onion slices and Brie cheese—all topped with their delicately spiced Creamy Pepper Dressing. It's just as easy on the palate as their Charleston Crabmeat Melt, although the latter, topped with tomatoes, Swiss cheese and alfalfa sprouts, offers a heartier lunch.

The next time I'm in town I'll dine in the upstairs dining room, which served as the main dwelling when this part of the home was reconstructed in 1886 after the earthquake. This dining area overlooks the garden and Raw Bar adjacent to the patio. The outdoor Raw Bar, as well as the patio enclosure, can be enjoyed throughout the winter due to a clever heating system built into their overhead canopies. You never have to give up the garden atmosphere.

For dinner, there is an exciting variety of continental cuisine with Low Country overtones. An excellent choice is the Fiddler Combination. The dish offers a melange of fresh seafood and mushrooms, sautéed in garlic butter and served over Rice Pilaf. If you prefer fewer calories, the Charleston

Extravaganza of steamed scallops, shrimp, oysters and clams will trick your weight scale.

When it was time to order dessert, we learned a little history that might explain how Lemon Chess Pie got its name. In the 1800s, when the kitchens were built apart from the main houses, pies were kept in a tin pie safe. The pie safe also was called a chest. But Southern accents dropped the "t," so pies were said to be kept in a "chess." Another version of the name's origin is that the household master asked what was cooking and heard, "Jes pies." Whatever the evolution of its name, one taste of their Lemon Chess convinced us that 82's recipe was a definite must for the book.

82 Queen is located at 82 Queen Street. Lunch is served from 11:30 a.m. until 2:30 p.m., and dinner is served from 5:30 p.m. until 10:30 p.m., Monday through Saturday. The Raw Bar is open from 4:00 p.m. For reservations (required for dinner and not accepted for lunch, except for large parties) call (803) 723-7591.

82 QUEEN'S LEMON CHESS PIE

1 pie shell
½ cup sugar
4 teaspoons cornstarch
2 teaspoons grated lemon
  peel

4 eggs, room temperature
⅓ cup lemon juice
5 tablespoons melted butter,
  cooled

Preheat oven to 400 degrees. Bake pie shell for about five minutes; remove it from the oven to cool. Reduce heat to 325 degrees. Combine sugar and cornstarch in a large bowl and mix, pressing out any lumps. Stir in the lemon peel. Beat in eggs, one at a time. Stir in lemon juice and blend in the butter. Pour the filling into the pie shell. Bake until puffed and golden brown, approximately 50 minutes. Cool before serving. The filling will thicken and fall somewhat, acquiring a jelly-like texture as it cools. Yields 1 pie.

82 QUEEN'S CHARLESTON CRABMEAT MELT

2 English muffins
8 ounces Crabmeat Imperial
(recipe below)

1 tomato, sliced into 8
pieces
8 slices Swiss cheese
½ cup alfalfa sprouts

Cut muffins in half and toast. Place 2 ounces of Crabmeat Imperial on each half. Top each with 2 tomato slices and 2 cheese slices. Bake at 450 degrees for 12 to 15 minutes. Serve sprouts on the side or on top. Serves 4.

Crabmeat Imperial:

2 tablespoons butter
½ bell pepper, diced
1 tablespoon diced onions
3 slices white bread
½ pound fresh white
crabmeat
1 tablespoon chopped
parsley

1 tablespoon fresh lemon
juice
⅛ cup chopped pimento
dash of Tabasco sauce
½ teaspoon dry mustard
½ teaspoon Worcestershire
sauce
salt and pepper to taste
¼ cup mayonnaise

Melt butter in a skillet and sauté peppers and onions until clear. Cut bread into small cubes. Combine all remaining ingredients with bread in a separate bowl, and toss lightly with peppers and onions.

NOTE: Crabmeat Imperial can be used to stuff shrimp, flounder or clams. It also can be served as an entrée. Bake in a casserole dish for 30 minutes at 325 degrees.

THE CHART HOUSE
Charleston

THE CHART HOUSE The Chart House is actually two identical buildings under one roof—perhaps a result of a problem that has plagued parents since time began. Could it have been sibling rivalry that led the wealthy Charleston merchant, Josiah Smith, to construct twin residences for his two sons in 1797? Whatever the reason, the building is soundly constructed. This sturdy historic structure stood fast against the famous earthquake of 1886. The double building stands today as a tribute to a wise father and master builder.

The spacious rooms of the restaurant are decorated in a nautical theme, attractively carried through with sailing artifacts and lots of gleaming brass. The Maritime Bar sports the motif of a waterfront pub. If the sailing photographs and wooden boat hulls on the walls fail to make a sailor out of you, perhaps the dining rooms on the upper levels will.

The nautical theme is not as prominent in the cuisine as you might expect. Meat and potato lovers will thoroughly enjoy the bill of fare, for the cuisine is typically American. Those preferring seafood or fowl dishes need not fret, for there are enough selections to please most palates. A field day awaits calorie counters at the impressive brass salad bar that features fifty to sixty items, depending on the season.

Not all of the restaurant carries nautical furnishings. The afternoon that Dawn and I dined at The Chart House, we were shown to a table in the Garden Room, where a hand-painted mural and ferns in hanging baskets gave us the feeling that we were sitting on a terrace. Three large, arched windows allowed us a view of the private courtyard below. We were told that this romantic patio area, complete with a fountain and candles at night, is a favorite strolling spot during the warmer months.

Even though we visited for lunch in December, the warm atmosphere of the Garden Room made us think of summer fare, so we selected salads with the House Dressing. The dressing is a creamy blend with a hint of celery, a perfect way to top off the crisp greens. Since we had a light lunch, we decided to go all out and ordered the Mud Pie. When the giant slabs of pie arrived, we couldn't believe our eyes. Each piece stood four or five inches high. The melt-in-your-mouth goodness of the coffee ice cream, packed in a chocolate cookie crust and topped with fudge sauce and whipped cream, has made The Chart House famous. We ate every bit of the delicious concoction and were rewarded with the recipe, which wowed our families as much as it did us.

Our trip to this historic restaurant concluded with a visit to the attic where supplies are stored and a ghost is said to make his home. This spirit is considered a "one-way ghost" because his shadow is always seen heading in the same direction. No one is sure of the identity of the spirit. My guess is that the footsteps heard in the attic storeroom belong to none other than Josiah Smith, who is still checking to see that all is well in his twin buildings.

The Chart House is located at 85–87 Broad Street in Charleston. Dinner is served from 6:00 p.m. until 10:00 p.m., Sunday through Thursday, and from 6:00 p.m. until 11:00 p.m. on Friday and Saturday. Reservations are not required, but the phone number is (803) 722–6182.

THE CHART HOUSE'S MUD PIE

1¼ cups crushed chocolate wafers
½ stick butter, melted
½ gallon coffee ice cream

1½ cups commercial fudge sauce
2 cups whipped cream
½ cup slivered almonds

Add crushed wafers to melted butter and mix well. Press mixture into a 9-inch pie plate. (You can substitute a commercial chocolate pie crust.) Fill wafer crust with softened ice cream. Freeze until ice cream is firm. Top with cold fudge sauce. Store in the freezer for approximately 10 hours. Serve on chilled dessert plates. Top with whipped cream and slivered almonds. Yields 1 pie.

THE CHART HOUSE'S SUN RICE

1 cup converted rice
1 tablespoon soy sauce
2 tablespoons butter
2 cups water
dash garlic
dash salt
¼ cup diced tomatoes

¼ cup finely chopped green
 peppers
¼ cup finely chopped green
 or red onions
1 tablespoon chopped fresh
 parsley

Combine all ingredients except vegetables in a greased casserole dish, mixing with a spoon until well blended. Cover and bake in a 375-degree oven until fully cooked, about 30 minutes. Remove from oven and mix in the four raw vegetables. Cover, and let sit for 5 minutes before serving. (The vegetables will steam slightly, but will maintain a crunchy consistency.)

THE CHART HOUSE'S BLUE CHEESE DRESSING

¾ cup sour cream
½ teaspoon dry mustard
½ teaspoon black pepper
½ teaspoon salt
⅓ teaspoon garlic powder

1 teaspoon Worcestershire
 sauce
1⅓ cups mayonnaise
½ cup Danish blue cheese

In a medium mixing bowl, combine sour cream, mustard, pepper, salt, garlic powder and Worcestershire sauce. Beat with an electric mixer for 2 minutes at low speed. Add mayonnaise, and blend for 30 seconds at low speed. Turn mixer to medium speed and blend for 2 more minutes. Crumble blue cheese into small pieces and add to mixture. Blend at low speed 2 to 3 minutes. Chill in refrigerator for 24 hours before serving. Yields 2½ cups.

THE EAST BAY TRADING
COMPANY
Charleston

THE EAST BAY TRADING COMPANY

Be prepared to be swept off your feet when you visit The East Bay Trading Company. This three-story 1880 warehouse is heady with early American charm. A collection of treasures gathered from all over the country abounds in this one-of-a-kind restaurant, located in Charleston's historic restoration district.

As soon as you spot the antique popcorn pushcart and old-time railroad station bench you will feel the urge to do some serious browsing. Why not start out, like we did, by ordering a drink inside the genuine San Francisco cable car? We sipped refreshing Strawberry Daiquiris and admired a Gay Nineties bicycle, an old fashioned gas pump and a ten foot high Victorian pier mirror on the wall next to the bar.

If you can drag yourself away from the entertaining first floor, fine dining awaits on the second and third levels of the restaurant. From the upper floors you will have a better view of the atrium and skylight that allow a flood of sunlight during the day and a cozy, under-the-stars feeling at night. Our table provided a close-up of the lush greenery that sprouts and tumbles from antique cooking pots suspended from the lofty ceiling.

The environment is not the only attraction at East Bay. The continental cuisine is an equal rival. We honestly didn't know where to begin with so many tempting offerings, so we asked the chef. We were delighted with his suggestions.

We were served Veal Stuffed Mushrooms topped with cream sauce and Snails in garlic butter for appetizers. You'd have thought we hadn't eaten in a week. My Casserole of Drunken Fishes, a crock full of steaming chunks of assorted seafood simmered in wine, was divine. Dawn's Linguine with Shrimp disappeared in a matter of minutes. For those interested in lighter fare, the menu lists several salad options, Stir-fried Vegetables and many broiled seafood selections.

We had no business ordering dessert, but who can resist rum-soaked Hot Austrian Apple Strudel or Cherry Kirsch Parfait? We couldn't, that's for sure.

On our way out, we decided on one more stop at the cable car. From our seats we were able to see the jazz ensemble, whose music we had admired throughout dinner. Entertainment is a nightly feature at this vibrant restaurant, with each evening devoted to beach music, folk music or jazz.

The East Bay Trading Company is located at 161 East Bay Street in Charleston. Lunch is served from 11:30 a.m. until 2:30 p.m., Monday through Friday. Dinner is served from 5:30 p.m. until 10:30 p.m., Monday through Thursday, and from 5:30 p.m. until 11:00 p.m. on Friday and Saturday. Winter hours may vary. For reservations (recommended) call (803) 722–0722.

THE EAST BAY TRADING COMPANY'S
STIR-FRIED VEGETABLES

3 tablespoons sesame oil
4 broccoli florets
1 small zucchini, sliced
1 small yellow squash,
  sliced
6 sliced mushroom caps
1 small carrot, sliced

4 cherry tomatoes
½ cup finely sliced red or
  white cabbage
½ cup chopped fresh
  spinach
½ cup sliced scallions
3 tablespoons soy sauce

In a very hot sauté pan or wok, combine sesame oil and all vegetables. Toss and cook for one minute, stirring constantly. Add soy sauce, tossing until well blended. (May be served over rice.) Serves 2 generously.

THE EAST BAY TRADING COMPANY'S
CHERRY KIRSCH PARFAIT

1 tablespoon commercial
  chocolate syrup
½ cup vanilla ice cream
5 bing cherries, seeded

½ cup chocolate ice cream
1 ounce cherry-flavored
  brandy
½ cup whipped cream

Cover the bottom of a parfait glass with chocolate syrup. Add vanilla ice cream and top with 4 cherries. Add chocolate ice cream and pour brandy over all. Top with whipped cream and garnish with a cherry. Serves 1.

THE EAST BAY TRADING COMPANY'S
LINGUINE WITH SHRIMP

6 ounces linguine	1 tablespoon fresh parsley
2 tablespoons butter	salt and white pepper to
½ tablespoon ground garlic	taste
4 ounces tiny shrimp	2 to 3 tablespoons Parmesan
½ ounce white wine	cheese

Cook linguine al dente. Rinse thoroughly with cold water and set aside. To a medium sauté pan, add butter, garlic and shrimp. Cook for one minute or until shrimp are done, adding the wine during the cooking process. Add linguine, parsley, salt, pepper and Parmesan cheese to shrimp, and toss thoroughly before serving. Serves 2.

FRENCH QUARTER RESTAURANT
AT THE LODGE ALLEY INN
Charleston

THE FRENCH QUARTER

The thought of an alley usually conjures up the image of a dark, mysterious and unattractive passageway. Not so at Lodge Alley. The ten-foot alley, paved with Belgian block down the middle and banked with granite on both sides, is typical of early eighteenth-century Charleston. It's not at all dark and ugly.

Karen and I would not have known about The French Quarter Restaurant if Charleston's restaurateurs had not recommended that we investigate. Our sleuthing led to the discovery that the alley is named after a 1773 Masonic Lodge where Charleston's Liberty Boys openly defied the British. On November 7, 1774, effigies of the pope, the devil, Lord North and Governor Thomas Hutchinson of Massachusetts were displayed on a "rolling stage" or parade float to protest the harsh treatment shown Boston.

We also discovered that the restaurant is called The French Quarter because this area was settled by French Huguenots, who arrived in 1680 with little more than their business skills and their faith.

Today's trés chic Lodge Alley was originally a warehouse that stored barrels of indigo, rice, salt beef and hams. It is fitting that much of the food stored there was considered exceptional, because we were told to investigate it precisely because of the fine cuisine to be found there today. It's true that exceptional food can be found throughout Charleston. But no other restaurant features a giant, open rotisserie imported from France to cook lamb, squab and other meats.

We were seated in an ivory-colored dining room appointed with simplified Corinthian columns. The fresh red roses in the silver bud vase gave our white linen tablecloth the perfect splash of color. We sampled a wonderful appetizer of Oysters en Brochette, prepared with bacon and served with a creamy mustard sauce. This was followed by a very rich and subtly seasoned Shrimp Bisque.

Karen chose the Veal la Louisiane, a combination of veal and seafood in a delicate Madeira sauce. I wanted to try something from the rotisserie and decided on their Swordfish au Beurre Rouge. It was fresh and basted to seduce any palate.

Their wine list includes over one hundred imported and domestic vintages, with an expected French dominance. What a decision! We chose a crisp chardonnay that was perfect.

That old axiom, "seeing is believing," does not apply here—tasting does! We shared a light Hazelnut Torte reminiscent of caramel. Ah, the French really have the last word when it comes to creamy desserts.

My last word on this renovated eighteenth-century warehouse is "hurrah," for that stalwart Save Charleston Foundation which refused to allow this historic structure to turn into a high-rise condominium.

The French Quarter Restaurant at The Lodge Alley Inn is located at 195 East Bay Street in Charleston. Meals are served daily. Breakfast is served from 7:00 a.m. until 10:30 a.m. Lunch is served from 11:30 a.m. until 2:30 p.m. Dinner is served from 6:00 p.m. until 10:00 p.m. For reservations (recommended for dinner) call (803) 722–1611.

THE FRENCH QUARTER RESTAURANT'S OYSTERS EN BROCHETTE

20 shelled oysters
1½ cups flour
salt and pepper to taste
3 eggs
2 cups crushed bread
    crumbs

5 slices bacon
1½ cups peanut oil
Beurre Blanc Sauce with
    Ancienne Mustard (recipe
    below)

Strain oysters. Season the flour with salt and pepper. Beat the eggs. Put each oyster into the flour, shake off the excess and dip in beaten eggs. Let excess egg drip off. Coat oysters with bread crumbs, and set aside. Cut bacon into square pieces. Place 5 oysters and 5 bacon pieces on a small wooden or metal skewer. Heat peanut oil in a deep fryer. Fry oysters and bacon until light brown. Serve on Beurre Blanc Sauce with Ancienne Mustard (recipe below). Serves 4.

Beurre Blanc Sauce with Ancienne Mustard:

¼ cup white wine
¼ cup white wine vinegar
½ tablespoon chopped
   shallots
1 small bay leaf
1 cup heavy cream

2 sticks salted butter
salt and white pepper to
   taste
1½ teaspoons Ancienne
   mustard powder

In a saucepan, combine the white wine, wine vinegar, shallots and bay leaf. Reduce over heat to ⅛ cup. Add cream and reduce to half. Gradually whip in small pieces of butter. Season with salt, white pepper and mustard. Remove the bay leaf. Serve the sauce under oysters. Yields 2 cups.

THE FRENCH QUARTER RESTAURANT'S SHRIMP BISQUE

2 tablespoons butter
1 pound shrimp shells
1 small onion, diced
1 carrot, diced
½ teaspoon chopped garlic
¼ cup brandy
1 quart Fish Fumet (see
   Index) or fish stock

1 tablespoon tomato paste
¼ cup raw rice
1 bay leaf
salt to taste
cayenne pepper to taste
4 to 6 tablespoons shrimp
   pieces
1 cup heavy cream

Melt butter in a large skillet or Dutch oven, and sauté shells, onions, carrots and garlic. Add brandy, Fish Fumet, tomato paste, rice and bay leaf. Simmer for 1 hour. Remove bay leaf. Strain off the shells with a fine strainer, and puree rice mixture in a blender until smooth. Return to the pan and season with salt, cayenne and shrimp pieces. Add heavy cream and heat only until blended. Serves 6 to 8.

HENRY'S
Charleston

HENRY'S

Omitting Henry's from our Charleston tour would be like leaving seafood out of Low Country fare. We wouldn't dream of it.

In 1932, Henry Hasselmeyer, a German immigrant, opened his restaurant in a former grocery store located across from the busy City Market. Although a tornado nearly demolished everything around it in 1938, the restaurant survived to be maintained by the members of the same family for more than fifty years. As Henry's fame increased, the restaurant grew also, and today it occupies three buildings. Henry's proudly claims that it is the oldest continuously operating restaurant in South Carolina. A portrait of the three generations of Hasselmeyers is located near the cash register.

The general atmosphere of this well-loved restaurant is one of good-natured informality. In the main dining room, where the grocery once stood, you can still see the markings from the grocery's counters on the black and white tiled floor. Many regular customers prefer to be served lunch or dinner in the relaxing lounge area. It is not surprising to see some of the city's most prominent restaurateurs enjoying a meal in one of the leather-like booths.

The main drawing card at Henry's is seafood, and you will find a variety of dishes that have kept customers coming back over the years. Many of the dishes that have made Henry's famous, such as Seafood a la Wando, are named after rivers in the area. There is such an extensive list of tempting offerings—be it food, wine or cocktails—diners have a difficult time making a choice.

Fortunately, I had been told that the Crabmeat Salad is a special luncheon treat at Henry's. When the plate arrived at my table, I was glad of the recommendation. Attractively arranged on a bed of lettuce, and garnished with peach slices, the crabmeat was just as it should be. There were no overpowering sauces or spices to mar its distinctive taste. Fresh raw Vegetables and Cheese Dip were accompanied with rolls and butter. If seafood is not your favorite fare, don't worry. Henry's aims to please all customers by offering a variety of beef, chops and fowl selections.

Prices at Henry's also make the restaurant popular. This is surely the place to bring the whole family, dine on scrumptious Low Country fare and, perhaps, have enough money leftover to enjoy the sights of Charleston. You'll find a map of the city's attractions on the back of the menu.

Henry's is located at 54 Market Street in Charleston. Meals are served from noon until 10:30 p.m., Monday through Saturday. Reservations are not accepted, but the telephone number is (803) 723-4363.

HENRY'S FLOUNDER A LA GHERARDI

Stuffing:
½ pound shrimp, cooked and deveined	2 tablespoons sherry
¼ cup crabmeat	4 tablespoons butter
¼ pound of bread, shredded	1 tablespoon fresh parsley
2 to 3 scallions, finely chopped	1 small egg
	salt and pepper to taste

Place all ingredients in a bowl and mix until thoroughly combined. Cover and refrigerate.

Flounder:
salt and pepper to taste	4 slices bacon
4 large flounder fillets	12 tiny shrimp, cleaned
16 ounces stuffing	12 green olives, chopped

Salt and pepper each fillet, and place 4 ounces of stuffing in the center of each. Fold the fillets over the stuffing. Spray the bottom of a large, flat dish with non-stick cooking spray. Place fillets in dish, and top each one with 3 shrimp, 3 olives and one strip of bacon. Cover and bake for 25 to 30 minutes at 400 degrees. Serves 4.

HENRY'S CAROLINA SHRIMP WITH CURRY

3 tablespoons butter
1 tart apple, chopped
1 stalk celery, chopped
1 medium onion, chopped
1 leek, chopped
2 teaspoons lemon juice
1 to 2 teaspoons curry
  powder
¼ teaspoon ginger
¼ teaspoon thyme

¼ teaspoon cayenne pepper
¼ teaspoon salt
1 tablespoon flour
1½ cups light cream
1½ pounds medium
  shrimp, deveined and
  cooked
3 cups cooked rice
commercial chutney for
  garnish

In a large skillet, melt the butter and sauté the apple, celery, onion and leek until transparent, about 5 minutes. Add lemon juice, curry powder, ginger, thyme, cayenne and salt. Slowly sprinkle in flour, then gradually pour in cream, stirring constantly. Reduce heat and continue to stir occasionally until sauce thickens. If sauce becomes too thick, add more cream, a tablespoon at a time, until desired consistency is reached. Add shrimp and simmer only until heated through. Serve over hot rice, and garnish with chutney. Serves 6.

HENRY'S FRIED GRITS

3 cups water
1 cup quick grits
½ teaspoon salt
2 eggs
¼ cup milk

2 cups well-ground cracker
  meal
2 to 3 tablespoons cooking
  oil

Boil water and add grits and salt. Stir to combine mixture. Cover and reduce heat to low. Continue cooking for 5 minutes, stirring occasionally. Remove from heat and spread grits into a 3-quart, oblong baking dish and let cool. When cool, cut into 4-inch squares. In a separate bowl, combine eggs and milk until incorporated. Dip each grit square into egg batter and coat with cracker meal. In a skillet, heat oil and fry squares until golden brown. Serves 6 to 8.

44

MARIANNE RESTAURANT
Charleston

**MARIANNE
RESTAURANT**

If this popular Charleston restaurant had been named by an American with a whim for patriotic titles, it might be known today as Uncle Sam's instead of Marianne. The proprietor, Serge Claire, is French born and bred, however, and he preferred to name the building after the female symbol of the Republic of France.

As you might expect, the restaurant's interior is representative of the owner's homeland. But don't expect an air of formality. Instead, you'll find the easygoing attitude of the country French in this historic structure dating back to the mid-1880s.

The Claires' extensive remodeling efforts have restored much of the building's original charm. The aged, English-style brick found on the restaurant's exterior and interior was removed, cleaned and replaced. It was during this mammoth renovation that a star was discovered in the ceiling. Apparently, the star is the symbol of the Daughters of the Confederacy, who once had occupied the building. According to Claire, the Daughters were so perturbed when they moved in and learned that the former tenants of the building were members of the Ku Klux Klan that a priest was called. The priest agreed that since it had been a meeting place for the Klan, a blessing was in order to rid the building of this taint.

The blessing was obviously well received, as Marianne Restaurant has become the "in" dining spot, especially for Le Brake Fast, a late supper which begins at 11:00 p.m. Lines form outside all the way around the corner to partake of the classic French cuisine at the popular after-theater hour.

Karen and I slipped in the side door, which opens into a most unusual bar of Japanese-lacquered ebony wood with mother-of-pearl inlays. You can look through a wrought iron grill beside the bar into an elaborate wine cellar. Naturally, fine French wines are featured, but there are interesting continental and domestic vintages as well.

We began our meal with a French drink called a Kir Royale. It was originally the creation of a bishop in the Dijon region of France, but Claire has substituted champagne for white wine. It's a recipe worth asking for.

We then enjoyed a unique pâté that could only have been made by a Frenchman, plus oysters with three preparations: Rockefeller, Bienville and Marianne. Everyone who sampled had a favorite, and mine was the Marianne.

This restaurant displays its individuality in a number of clever ways, such as the hand-carved mushroom accenting our entrée of Red Snapper Marianne. This absolutely scrumptious dish could easily be a prize dieting choice as it is poached in white wine. Just skip the cream sauce that tops the fish if you are thinking of lighter fare.

It was impossible to think of lighter fare when we saw the desserts, so we didn't even try. Instead we shared a Mousse de Marron Christine that delivered everything its appearance promised.

Marianne Restaurant is located at 235 Meeting Street in Charleston. Dinner is served from 6:00 p.m. until 10:30 p.m., and Le Brake Fast is served from 11:00 p.m. until 1:30 a.m., Monday through Saturday. For reservations (required for dinner but not accepted for Le Brake Fast) call (803) 722–7196.

MARIANNE RESTAURANT'S RED SNAPPER

Fish Fumet:

1 pound fish bones	1 tablespoon fresh parsley
1 ounce white wine	1 teaspoon white pepper
1 gallon water	1 to 2 teaspoons salt
1 medium onion, sliced	½ lemon, cut up
1 shallot, chopped	

Place fish bones in a Dutch oven, and moisten with wine. Add water, onion slices, shallots, parsley, pepper, salt and lemon. Bring to a boil. Reduce heat and simmer 3 to 4 hours until liquid is reduced to ¼ of original volume. Strain bones, and reserve liquid.

Sauce a la Bonne Femme:

5 tablespoons butter	1 cup sliced mushrooms
½ cup diced onions	1 tablespoon lemon juice
⅓ cup diced shallots	1 cup white wine
2 tablespoons flour	salt and white pepper to
1 cup milk	taste
¼ cup Fish Fumet	½ to 1 cup heavy cream

In a small skillet, melt 3 tablespoons of butter. Sauté onions and shallots until translucent. In a separate saucepan, combine flour and milk, stirring to make a roux. Add remaining butter to make a sauce. Add ¼ cup Fish Fumet to the sauce, and stir. Add sautéed onions and shallots, mushrooms, lemon juice, wine, salt and white pepper. Let simmer 10 to 15 minutes. Stir half of heavy cream into mixture. Taste, and add remainder for richer sauce, if desired.

Court Bouillon:

1 quart Fish Fumet	1 tablespoon lemon juice
1 cup white wine	4 7-ounce red snapper fillets
1 shallot, chopped	parsley for garnish
1 small onion, chopped	

Place all ingredients except snapper and parsley in a large heavy skillet on medium-high heat. Stir until ingredients are combined. Add snapper and poach a few minutes until tender and flaky. Remove snapper to warm plates and generously cover with hot Sauce a la Bonne Femme. Garnish with parsley. Serves 4.

MARIANNE RESTAURANT'S KIR ROYALE

1 tablespoon creme de cassis	4 to 5 ounces dry champagne
	¼ slice orange for garnish

In a champagne glass, add creme de cassis and champagne. Stir. Garnish with an orange slice. Serves 1.

MIDDLETON PLACE RESTAURANT
Charleston

**MIDDLETON PLACE
RESTAURANT**

When I was a teenager growing up in the Southwest, I spent hours daydreaming about what it would be like to be a Southern belle and live on some far-off grand and glorious plantation. Perhaps you can understand the feelings that engulfed me, then, as I arrived at Middleton Place, a magnificent 5,000-acre antebellum plantation bordering the Ashley River. This plantation seemed to me the embodiment of my dreams.

Very few restaurants can claim a setting as romantic as the Middleton Place Restaurant, located at the end of a breathtaking tour of America's oldest, and perhaps most elegant, landscaped gardens. History reports that one hundred slaves toiled for a decade to complete the terraced lawns, walks, artificial lakes and formal gardens that were designed by Henry Middleton in 1741. Although the historic plantation has been ravaged by war, fire and earthquake, the gardens have survived unharmed, though at times untended. No wonder the "little gray lady," a disgruntled spirit sometimes seen wandering aimlessly about the neglected gardens, could find no peace until restoration efforts began in 1916.

The restaurant, built around 1930, is a replica of the plantation's original rice mill. A seat on the enclosed porch offers a breathtaking view of azaleas, which bloom by the thousands along the banks of the mill pond in the spring and summer.

If you can tear your eyes away from the floral wonderland and focus on the restaurant's menu, you will find a listing of typical plantation fare. What could be more representative of the Low Country than Hoppin' John, a spicy mixture of black-eyed peas, bacon and rice? Perhaps you'd like to try the Smoked Ham with Charleston Red Rice, or Ham Biscuits and Okra Gumbo. Top off your meal with a generous serving of Huguenot Torte, which, I was told, is made from a 250-year-old recipe. This delicious, crusty apple and pecan cake is served smothered with whipped cream and topped with a cherry. I do declare—however did those Southern belles maintain such tiny waists with such bountiful temptations?

For those of us concerned with our own spreading waistlines, the menu offers a fresh Spinach Salad and She-crab Soup. A pot of tea, served by long-skirted waitresses, was the perfect beverage for my plantation luncheon. To say I was reluctant to leave this charming restaurant—with its brick-tiled floors, cypress-paneled walls and red chintz tablecloths—would be an understatement. I plan to return again, perhaps for one of those special antebellum dinners at which guests are made to feel as if they are dining in the aristocratic elegance of eighteenth-century plantation life.

Middleton Place Restaurant is located 14 miles northwest of Charleston on Highway 61. Lunch is served from 11:00 a.m. until 3:00 p.m., Tuesday through Sunday. Dinner is served at 7:00 p.m. on Friday and Saturday evenings, by reservation only. The telephone number is (803) 556–6024.

MIDDLETON PLACE RESTAURANT'S
HUGUENOT TORTE

2 eggs, room temperature
1¼ cups sugar
¼ cup sifted flour
2½ teaspoons baking
   powder
¼ teaspoon salt
1 teaspoon vanilla

1 cup chopped tart apples
1 cup chopped pecans
1 cup heavy cream,
   whipped
8 maraschino cherries
   (optional)

Beat eggs until frothy and light lemon-colored. Add sugar gradually to eggs, beating on low speed of electric mixer. Add flour, baking powder and salt; beat at medium speed. Add vanilla and fold in apples and pecans. Pour mixture into a well-buttered 8-inch by 12-inch baking pan. Bake at 325 degrees for 30 to 40 minutes until mixture is crusty and brown. To serve, scoop up with a pancake turner, keeping crusty part on top. Top each serving with a large dollop of whipped cream. Add a maraschino cherry to each serving as a garnish, if you like. Serves 8.

MIDDLETON PLACE RESTAURANT'S
CHARLESTON RED RICE

¼ pound bacon, chopped
½ cup diced onions
⅓ cup diced green peppers
1 cup water

1 8-ounce can tomato sauce
1 teaspoon brown sugar
¼ teaspoon salt
1 cup uncooked rice

In a saucepan, sauté bacon, onions and green peppers until tender. Add water, tomato sauce, brown sugar and salt. Bring to a boil and add the rice. Reduce heat, cover and simmer for 15 minutes. Remove from heat and let stand, covered, for 5 minutes before serving. Serves 6.

MIDDLETON PLACE RESTAURANT'S
GINGER CARROTS

8 to 10 peeled carrots
¼ cup honey
¼ cup margarine
1 teaspoon salt

½ teaspoon ground ginger
¼ teaspoon ground
cinnamon

Slice carrots diagonally. Simmer in a covered saucepan in a small amount of water (½ cup) for 5 minutes. Drain carrots and combine with remaining ingredients. Simmer in saucepan until tender. Serves 6.

PERDITA'S
Charleston

PERDITA'S

It's no wonder such an unforgettable woman as Perdita should merit a restaurant bearing her name. This celebrated English actress and mistress to the Prince of Wales was the toast of Europe in the late 1700s. She even managed to set a few records in colonial America.

Legend has it that when the famous beauty performed on the Charleston stage, she caused quite a stir. Apparently, a local gentleman didn't think much of the caliber of her acting. Another man, a poet who was quite smitten with Perdita, was offended by this slight to her abilities, and a duel was arranged. It was a fight to death. This gave Charleston the dubious distinction of being the only South Carolina city to have a death resulting from a duel. The ghost of the ill-fated loser reportedly still roams about the city in search of his beloved Perdita.

Located in a pink, two-story building, Perdita's has been part of the Charleston scene for over 200 years. Like its namesake, the restaurant has earned international acclaim. The architecture is referred to as "turn-of-the-century Charleston" by the Bennett family, who has operated the restaurant for over fifty years.

A quiet air of intimacy exists in each of the three distinctive dining rooms and also in the upstairs lounge. Featured in the main dining room is a large wine cellar. A vast collection of fine wines can be seen through the wrought iron gates at the cellar's entrance. It came as no surprise to find that the restaurant's wine list fills six pages.

Since I was in Charleston, I decided to do as the Charlestonians do and ordered seafood. I was glad that I followed my hunch, because the Baked Crabmeat Remick, smothered with a spicy chili sauce, was superb. Next came the Alaskan King Crab Alphonse swimming in a lemon butter sauce. Beef and fowl lovers need not despair since a tempting variety of non-seafood dishes is available for them.

When the twenty-two item dessert menu arrived, I was truly at a loss. Each mouth-watering offering seemed too good to pass up. I requested the favorite of the house and was served a wedge of Sté. Honoree Pie. This light, brandy-flavored custard concoction was a perfect ending to a gracious meal.

It is difficult to forget an evening spent at this restaurant, which never lets you dismiss from your memory its romantic namesake, Perdita. Her portrait hangs on the wall, and her silhouette adorns the burgundy-banded china.

Perdita's is located at 10 Exchange Street in Charleston. From March through June, dinner is served from 6:00 p.m. until 9:00 p.m., Monday through Saturday. During the months of July through February, dinner is served at the same hours, Tuesday through Saturday. For reservations (recommended) call (803) 577–4364.

PERDITA'S ALASKAN KING CRAB ALPHONSE

½ cup mayonnaise
1 tablespoon catsup
2 teaspoons lemon juice
1 teaspoon parsley
2 teaspoons minced chives

2 tablespoons brandy
pinch of granulated garlic
1 stick butter
1 pound Alaskan king
    crabmeat

Combine all the ingredients except butter and crabmeat in a bowl, and mix thoroughly. Melt butter in a saucepan; add the crabmeat and the mayonnaise mixture. Heat thoroughly over medium heat and serve. (This dish may be served over hot, cooked rice, if desired.) Serves 4.

PERDITA'S BAKED CRABMEAT REMICK

1 pound crabmeat
1 teaspoon dry mustard
½ teaspoon paprika
½ teaspoon celery salt
dash Tabasco sauce

½ cup chili sauce
1 teaspoon tarragon vinegar
1¾ cups mayonnaise
4 cups cooked rice
8 strips crisp, cooked bacon

Place crabmeat in a buttered baking dish. Bake at 325 degrees for 15 to 20 minutes until heated through. Meanwhile, combine all remaining ingredients except rice and bacon in a bowl and mix well. Remove the crab from the oven and spread the mayonnaise sauce over warmed crabmeat. Return it to the oven, and broil until the sauce is glazed. Spoon the crab over rice, and top with bacon strips. Serves 4.

PERDITA'S STÉ. HONOREE PIE

1 envelope unflavored
  gelatin
1½ cups milk
3 eggs, separated
⅓ cup chopped raisins
3 tablespoons ground
  almonds
1 cup finely ground
  macaroon crumbs
½ cup grated chestnuts in
  syrup (commercial)

1 teaspoon vanilla
2 tablespoons brandy
⅛ teaspoon salt
⅓ cup sugar
1 9-inch, deep dish pie
  shell, baked
1 pint fresh, whole
  strawberries
1 cup whipped cream

Soften gelatin in ¼ cup milk. Scald remaining milk in a double boiler. Beat egg yolks slightly with a fork and add to warm milk, stirring constantly over heat until the mixture coats a wooden spoon. Add the gelatin mix, raisins, almonds, macaroon crumbs, chestnuts, vanilla, brandy and salt to milk mixture. Chill until filling begins to set. Beat egg whites on high speed of an electric mixer, adding sugar while beating. Fold egg white mixture into chilled mixture, and pour into a baked pie shell. Chill until firm. Before serving, spread a layer of strawberries over the entire pie, and spoon whipped cream over the berries. Yields 1 pie.

NOTE: One 4-ounce jar of brandied fruit may be used in place of raisins, almonds, macaroon crumbs, chestnuts, vanilla and brandy.

PHILIPPE MILLION RESTAURANT
Charleston

PHILIPPE MILLION RESTAURANT

Since archaeologists didn't find the set of false teeth George Washington lost while dining at McCrady's Tavern, it's doubtful that you will either. He dined in the Long Room, located just above where Philippe Million Restaurant is located today. At the opposite end of the Long Room is the oldest known theater in America, complete with a raked stage and pulleys for flying scenery. Our president's diary, dated May 4, 1791, recorded that "a very sumptuous dinner" was consumed here, after which artillery fire followed each of sixteen toasts.

Washington did not describe the menu, but archaeologists discovered from artifacts that this restaurant was then, as it is today, a very high-profile place to dine. Apparently, during colonial times mutton was served only in the better restaurants. So when mutton bones and wine labels from premium vintages were discovered, researchers were certain of the former tavern's character. It's especially appropriate that wine labels provided a crucial key to the archaeologists, because Philippe Million, the creator of the new restaurant in the same location, is an internationally acclaimed wine connoisseur.

Million's choice of a location for his restaurant illustrates the philosophy the French have toward food. Million believes that the plate is to the palate what the stage is to an audience. "Fine French cooking is, in short, good theater," he says. What better place could Million have chosen than a posh tavern that includes a stage?

In a sense, it was curtain time from the moment Karen and I entered the restaurant through the brick courtyard. We were seated opposite a dramatic 1756 Aubusson tapestry. Act One began when the crystal candelabra on our table was lighted and we were presented with a Lobster Salad flowered with beets. Color is a key element in French cuisine, and our salads were a kaleidoscope of bright hues. We wondered if the lobster could possibly taste as divine as it appeared. It did, prompting a spontaneous toast to our chefs with a Chateau Carbonnieux.

Action usually occurs during the second act, so we trouped back to the kitchen to watch the new, low-calorie method of preparing Breast of Duck with Bordeaux. If I'm half as skillful at home, my rendition will be the best duck my family has ever tasted. Of course, when you visit the restaurant, you don't have to do anything but sit and be pampered by the excellent food and service to thoroughly enjoy Act Two.

Act Three was a dazzling finale that is called Symphony of Desserts. The beautifully arranged tray, filled with French delicacies, exotic fruits and petite pastries, was a triumph. It's the first time I've witnessed and participated in clapping for the chefs in a restaurant. Why not? It was a delicious production of nouvelle cuisine at its ultimate.

Philippe Million Restaurant is located at 2 Unity Alley in Charleston. Dinner is served from 6:30 p.m. until 9:30 p.m., Tuesday through Sunday. For reservations (preferred) call (803) 577–7472.

PHILIPPE MILLION RESTAURANT'S CHARLOTTE AUX POIRES A L'EAU DE FRAMBOISE
(Raspberry Mousse)

1 cup milk	3 ounces raspberry brandy
1 teaspoon vanilla	½ pint whipping cream
5 egg yolks	1 package lady fingers
½ cup sugar	1 square semisweet
1 teaspoon unflavored	chocolate
gelatin	

In a large saucepan, boil the milk with the vanilla. Remove from heat. Add the egg yolks and sugar; beat until mixed. Return mixture to heat and add gelatin. Cook until mixture reaches slightly thick consistency. Add the raspberry brandy and stir until mixed. Remove from heat and cool to room temperature. Refrigerate until chilled. Whip the cream, and gently fold it into the chilled mixture until well combined. Line the sides of a 1½-quart serving bowl with lady fingers. Spoon mixture into the bowl and refrigerate for 12 hours. Shave chocolate over top before serving. Serves 6 to 8.

PHILIPPE MILLION RESTAURANT'S SUPREME DE CANETTE A LA LIE DU VIN
(Breast of Duck with Bordeaux)

1 4- to 5-pound duck
1 cup red Bordeaux wine
1 teaspoon red wine vinegar
1 cup chicken stock or
  commercial chicken broth
1 tablespoon rosemary
1 pound fresh spinach,
  washed, destemmed and
  drained
6 to 8 carrots, julienned

2 medium zucchini, sliced
1 10-ounce package frozen
  French green beans
4 tablespoons butter
2 slices bacon, minced
⅛ teaspoon basil
pinch of salt
2 tablespoons vegetable oil
4 twists white pepper
parsley for garnish

Puncture duck with a fork at 2- to 4-inch intervals. Roast at 350 degrees until not quite done. Meanwhile, heat wine to 80 degrees for 5 minutes. Pour the wine back into the bottle or container and the residue will separate. Skim the wine residue and place 1 cup of residue in a saucepan. Reduce over high heat until ¼ cup remains. Add red wine vinegar and reduce slightly. Add chicken stock; reduce liquids by half and set the sauce aside.

Place rosemary in boiling water. Add spinach and cook a few seconds. Remove spinach from water and set aside to drain. Add carrots, zucchini and green beans to rosemary water and steam until barely tender. Drain and set aside.

Slice roasted duck into thin strips and set aside. In a skillet, melt 1 tablespoon butter. Add bacon and sauté spinach; remove. Add a tablespoon of butter and the basil and salt to the skillet. Sauté steamed zucchini, carrots and green beans. Add the 2 remaining tablespoons of butter and the oil to the skillet, blending until mixed. Sauté the duck and remove.

Arrange duck, spinach, zucchini, carrots and green beans equally on four plates. Add a twist of white pepper to each dish. Set in a 500-degree oven for 1 minute. Remove plates from the oven and ladle Bordeaux sauce over the duck and the vegetables. Garnish with parsley. Serves 4.

POOGAN'S PORCH
Charleston

POOGAN'S PORCH   Even though it was December, I sat on Poogan's front porch with a Peppermint Pattie, a delicious, chocolaty cocktail. Because of the mild Charleston climate, lucky guests can enjoy the restaurant's porches throughout most of the year.

Inside, Karen joined me for lunch in a room thought to have been the parlor in this 1891 residence. The white fireplace and moldings accentuate the room's dramatic, deep blue walls. The fresh daisies on our table and the camaraderie we noticed between waiters and guests gave this restaurant a relaxed, friendly atmosphere.

While trying to decide what to order, we decided to splurge with a bottle of Domaine Chandon champagne. I agree with the legendary creator of champagne, Dom Perignon, who said, "Champagne is like drinking stars." I've found few dishes that are not enhanced by a dry champagne.

Our sparkling wine certainly agreed with the appetizers, a creamy Low Country Pâté and the succulent Crabmeat a la Poogan's. Karen ordered the Scallops Savannah, a wondrous creation in a mustard wine sauce. I had their Santee Catfish. If you've never tried catfish, allow their chef to introduce you to this special preparation.

Supposedly, there is a female ghost who resides in the upstairs bar, which may have once been her bedroom. We took dessert here, hoping the spirit, reportedly a small old lady dressed in a black dress with a white lace collar, would join us. Maybe we were too preoccupied with the divine Bread Pudding with Bourbon Sauce to notice her. It is said that she appears, then vanishes just as quickly without speaking a word. We weren't too disappointed, as we'd been told she won't appear to guests.

We meandered out on the upstairs porch and decided that the next time we visit, we'll sit here. Perhaps we'll see Joanne Woodward and Paul Newman strolling down the lamp-lighted street. Poogan's is one of their favorite Charleston restaurants.

Poogan's Porch is located at 72 Queen Street in Charleston. Lunch is served from 11:30 a.m. until 2:30 p.m., Monday through Saturday. Dinner is served from 5:30 p.m. until 10:00 p.m., Sunday through Thursday, and from 5:30 p.m. until 11:00 p.m. on Friday and Saturday. Sunday brunch is served from 11:30 a.m. until 2:30 p.m. For reservations (recommended) call (803) 577–2337.

POOGAN'S PORCH'S BREAD PUDDING
WITH BOURBON SAUCE

Bread Pudding:

½ loaf day-old bread	1 stick butter, melted
½ cup raisins	¾ cup sugar
1 teaspoon cinnamon	2 eggs
1 teaspoon nutmeg	2 cups milk

Break or cut bread into large chunks. Place it in a baking dish and add raisins, cinnamon, nutmeg and butter. Mix together until well blended. In a small bowl, beat sugar and eggs with a whisk or electric mixer until well combined. Heat the milk, but do not boil. Add egg mixture to hot milk, mixing well. Add bread mixture and stir until well mixed. Pour everything into a greased casserole dish. Place the dish in a large roasting pan. Fill the roasting pan with water half way up the casserole dish, taking care not to get any water in the casserole. Bake at 350 degrees for 1 hour.

Bourbon Sauce:

2 sticks butter	1 egg
1 cup confectioners' sugar	2 tablespoons bourbon

Melt butter in a medium saucepan. Add sugar and cook, stirring constantly until glossy. Remove from heat. Whip in the egg with a whisk. Add the bourbon and stir until well blended. Pour about ¼ cup of sauce over each serving of Bread Pudding. Serves 4 generously.

POOGAN'S PORCH'S CRABMEAT A LA POOGAN'S

Crabmeat Spread:

½ pound crabmeat
1 tablespoon Worcestershire
  sauce
1 teaspoon dry mustard
1 egg

½ of crumbled biscuit
½ teaspoon salt
½ teaspoon white pepper
1 teaspoon chopped parsley

Combine all ingredients in a bowl and mix thoroughly. Cover and refrigerate until needed.

3 tablespoons butter
8 sliced mushroom caps
4 sliced artichoke hearts
Crabmeat Spread

½ cup white wine
4 large biscuits or English
  muffins, sliced in two and
  toasted

Melt butter and sauté mushrooms, artichokes and crabmeat mixture. Add white wine and mix until well blended and hot. Reduce heat until mixture thickens. Serve over toasted biscuits or muffins. Serves 4.

POOGAN'S PORCH'S PEPPERMINT PATTIE

½ ounce peppermint
  schnapps
½ ounce Kahlúa
½ ounce crème de cacao

2 ounces heavy cream
sprig of fresh mint for
  garnish

Place all ingredients except the mint in a blender, and mix until frothy. Serve over ice and garnish with a sprig of mint. Serves 1.

THE WINE CELLAR
AND THE COLONY HOUSE
Charleston

THE WINE CELLAR
THE COLONY HOUSE

It's too bad that a city—no matter how exotic or romantic—often loses its charm after you've lived in it for a while. Karen and I are glad we don't live in Charleston, because we don't ever want this city to lose its special appeal.

During a recent visit, we turned off a cobblestoned street and parked across from the harbor, where we could watch the dwindling activity as the day slipped over the horizon. Charleston's wharf area has undergone sophisticated maritime changes but, to my thinking, one of the most clever transitions is the conversion of the 1830s warehouse on Prioleau Street. When Charleston entered her golden era this warehouse held tons of the famous golden grain rice, indigo and cotton. All were exchanged for exotic spices and silk imports. Under the same warehouse roof today, there are two separate restaurants: The Colony House and The Wine Cellar.

Karen and I peeked through The Wine Cellar's window and saw racks of green wine bottles. Moments later, seated in high-backed leather chairs, we began our dinner with an appetizer of Shrimp in a tangy honey mustard sauce while sipping a young wine labeled Beaujolais Nouveau, which we chose from their extensive wine list.

The Wine Cellar is noted for its classical French cuisine. The seven-course dinner menu continually changes, but perhaps you'll have the good fortune to find their celebrated Monkfish creation available when you dine.

When you walk into The Colony House, only steps away from The Wine Cellar, the feeling is one of crossing to another continent. Representing the essence of Old Charleston, the décor echoes that of the sherbet-colored houses of the historic district. The atmosphere provides a charming backdrop to the New American cuisine, which is making swift inroads with gourmets.

We sat in Charleston-styled chairs and admired the flowers topping our linen tablecloth while we sampled Conch Fritters accompanied with a sweet-and-sour sauce, which is a great recipe for cocktail parties. We then traded bites of the Shrimp Provencale and the Veal Medallions with Raspberry Sauce. It would be difficult to award a blue ribbon to only one, but the shrimp is certainly lighter in calories.

Continent hopping for dessert, we returned to The Wine Cellar and enjoyed a most unusual Chocolate Soufflé. It reminded us of a hot, creamy pudding with a crunchy crust. It was a memorable finale to a romantic evening in this enchanting city.

The Wine Cellar and The Colony House are located at 35 Prioleau Street in Charleston. Dinner is served in The Wine Cellar from 6:30 p.m. until 10:00 p.m., Monday through Saturday. The Colony House serves lunch from 11:30 a.m. until 3:00 p.m., and dinner from 5:30 p.m. until 10:30 p.m., Monday through Saturday. The Colony House serves dinner on Sunday from 5:00 p.m. until 9:00 p.m. Reservations are recommended for both restaurants. The Wine Cellar's number is (803) 723–9463. The Colony House's is (803) 723–3424.

THE COLONY HOUSE'S CONCH FRITTERS

¾ cup conch meat, ground or very finely chopped
2 eggs
1½ teaspoons baking powder
¾ cup flour
½ teaspoon salt

2 tablespoons diced onions
2 tablespoons diced bell peppers
1 teaspoon chopped jalapeño peppers
oil for deep frying

Combine all ingredients except oil in a bowl until well mixed. In a heavy skillet or deep fryer, heat oil to 325 or 350 degrees. Drop tablespoonfuls of batter into the oil, varying the size to suit your purpose (small for appetizers, large for side dishes). Turn fritters as they rise to the surface, and fry until golden brown and cooked through. Serve with your favorite sauce. Serves 4.

THE WINE CELLAR'S VEAL MEDALLIONS
WITH RASPBERRY SAUCE

2 large onions, sliced
1 teaspoon salt
freshly ground pepper to
taste
2 cups chicken stock (or
commercial chicken
broth)
½ cup raspberry vinegar
1 cup heavy cream
1½ pounds veal loin cut
into 8 3-ounce medallions

1 tablespoon all-purpose
flour
2 tablespoons unsalted,
clarified butter
½ cup dry white wine
1½ cups fresh or frozen
raspberries
2 cups veal stock (or
commercial beef broth)

Season the onions with half of the salt and a little pepper. Combine onions, chicken stock and raspberry vinegar (reserving one tablespoon of vinegar) in a medium saucepan. Cover the pan, and cook over moderate to high heat until liquid has evaporated, about 15 minutes.

Put cream in a small saucepan and reduce volume until 3 tablespoons remain. Add the cooked onions to cream and bring to a boil. Remove onions from heat and keep in a warm oven.

Season the veal with remaining salt and pepper to taste; dust with flour on both sides. Heat the clarified butter in a heavy skillet and sauté veal until golden brown on both sides, but still pink inside. Remove and keep warm in oven.

Pour butter from the skillet, and deglaze skillet with the remaining raspberry vinegar and reduce until almost dry. Add wine to skillet and reduce until ⅓ of it remains. Add 1 cup raspberries (saving ½ cup for garnish) and veal or beef stock; reduce to 1 cup. Strain sauce to remove seeds, and pour over medallions. Garnish with the cooked, sliced onions and the raspberries. Serves 4.

THE ANCHORAGE HOUSE
Beaufort

THE ANCHORAGE
HOUSE

When I arrived at The Anchorage House, an imposing antebellum mansion overlooking the Beaufort River, I thought it a perfect setting for a historical romance novel. Built in the 1770s as a summer home for a wealthy Port Royal plantation owner, this elegant, three-tiered structure epitomizes the gracious lifestyle of the Old South. History even provides a ready-made cast of characters, including a ghost who refuses to leave the attic.

The touches of oriental craftsmanship and the military themes in the mansion's interior result from the redecorating completed by Admiral and Mrs. Lester Beardslee, who purchased the mansion in 1891. Secret wall panels, which you can inspect during your visit, once hid the admiral's passion—Cherry Bounces. His overindulgence in the spirited brew is reportedly the reason the original circular stairway, a treacherous affair for a tipsy admiral, was replaced with the current L-shaped oak one. Do you suppose the ghost traipsing about the attic is none other than Mrs. Beardslee, searching for the admiral's intoxicating cache?

I arrived at The Anchorage House late in the afternoon. It was an awkward time: too early for dinner but just right for appetizers and a Cherry Bounce. While waiting to be served in the bright white and gold dining room, I applauded the present owners, Vicki and Stig Jorgensen, for retaining the mansion's gracious and elegant ambiance.

The cuisine reflects the Danish influence of the chef's homeland. The Gravad Lax, an open-faced sandwich of marinated, homecured salmon slices atop a thin pumpernickel slice, is delicious. The accompanying mustard and dill sauce adds a bit of zip. If you're a liver lover, you must try the Fowl Liver Pâté, a combination of chicken and duck livers with sautéed mushrooms. Either hors d'oeuvre blends well with the admiral's cherry home brew.

You'll find an ample selection of menu items to tempt you, including the Supreme of Duckling Muscadine, a favorite of the house and a dish you can duplicate from the recipe the chef shared with me. An extensive wine list is available, and a special "from the pantry" section on the luncheon menu will please the diet-conscious and those wishing lighter meals.

Dessert was not in my plan, but when the Almond Mousse arrived, my willpower dissolved. The light and refreshing confection is a specialty dessert that is served with the four-course Anchorage House Dinner.

The Anchorage House is located at 1103 Bay Street in Beaufort and is open Monday through Saturday. Lunch is served from 11:30 a.m. until 2:00 p.m. Dinner is served from 6:00 p.m. until 9:30 p.m. For reservations (recommended) call (803) 524–9392.

THE ANCHORAGE HOUSE'S BUTTERMILK SOUP

3 egg yolks	juice of 3 lemons
½ cup sugar	pinch of nutmeg
1 quart buttermilk	5 cups chopped fresh fruit

Whip egg yolks with sugar until thick and pale yellow in color. Gradually blend in buttermilk, lemon juice and nutmeg. Chill until slightly thickened, approximately 2 to 3 hours. To serve, arrange half a cup of fruit in each of 10 bowls. Pour soup over top of each. Serves 10.

THE ANCHORAGE HOUSE'S
SUPREME OF DUCKLING MUSCADINE

1 4- to 5-pound duckling	1 tablespoon cornstarch
½ cup duckling drippings	¾ cup commercial
1 cup dry red wine	muscadine sauce
1 cup beef broth	

Pierce duckling with fork at 2- to 4-inch intervals. Roast in a 350-degree oven until ½ cup of drippings appear, approximately 15 to 20 minutes. Remove drippings and reserve.

Continue to roast duckling until done, approximately 1½ hours.

In a saucepan, combine skimmed drippings and wine, and cook over medium heat until reduced by ⅓. Add beef broth, cornstarch and muscadine sauce, and cook until well blended, about 20 minutes. Strain sauce mixture to remove lumps. To serve, spoon a dollop of sauce on each plate and top with cooked duckling slices. Serves 4.

THE ANCHORAGE HOUSE'S CHERRY BOUNCE

1½ ounces cherry liqueur
½ ounce vodka

1 tablespoon cherry juice from maraschino cherry jar
1 maraschino cherry

Fill a 6-ounce glass with crushed ice. Add liquid ingredients (do not stir) and top with cherry. Serves 1.

JOHN CROSS TAVERN
Beaufort

JOHN CROSS TAVERN

No, the father of our country did not sleep at John Cross Tavern, but you can be sure he was a frequent topic of conversation in this historic structure. Parson Weems, storyteller and author of *The Life of Washington*, is said to have taken his last breath here in 1825, perhaps after entertaining guests with a presidential tale.

Two restaurants can be found today in this building, which dates back to the early 1700s. Downstairs, at Harry's Restaurant, breakfast and lunch are served in an unpretentious, home-like setting. This inviting room was first a mercantile store and later was used as a schoolroom during the Revolutionary War period. The lower level is named after the building's owner, Harry Chakides. He assured me that I needn't worry about the floor falling in this 250-year-old structure. When he climbed under the structure twenty years ago, he discovered four layers of flooring. He added two more layers, bringing the total to six. Solid footing, indeed.

John Cross Tavern occupies the upper level of the colonial building. Formerly an inn, the tavern takes its name from the man whose signature appears on the original 1717 property grant. The bar is the perfect place for pre-dinner browsing. A glass case standing beside the original fireplace holds a collection of old bottles and clay pipes Mr. Chakides found on the grounds. I was curious about the reason for the various lengths of the pipes. He explained that it was common for the eighteenth-century smoker to simply break off a piece of pipe after each use to provide a sanitary mouthpiece for the next man.

The dining room, added to the structure during the 1970s, also contains interesting artifacts. Framed *Harper's Weekly* cartoons, dating back to the 1860s, line the walls and are illuminated at night by hurricane candle lamps.

We noticed such unusual items on the tavern's menu as Broiled Dolphin and Fried Quail. Although we were tempted to experiment, we opted for more familiar fare. Soup was our first course, and we each felt that our own particular selection

74

was the best. I'll let you judge whether the She-crab Soup, the Corn Chowder or the Clam Chowder takes the prize. Next came a trip to the salad bar, where each of us put together a satisfying mound of greens and toppings. When dinner came, I noticed that my teen-aged son, Sean, managed to polish off his Scallops and Fried Potatoes with his usual gusto. Ten-year-old Justin was thrilled to find that his child's plate of Rib Eye Steak and Fries was as large as many adult portions served in other restaurants.

We agreed to schedule our next visit to John Cross Tavern during the warm summer months, when we would be able to dine on the back terrace that overlooks the busy Beaufort River and the City Marina, a popular stopping point for Intracoastal Waterway travelers.

John Cross Tavern is located at 812 Bay Street in Beaufort. Breakfast and lunch are served at Harry's Restaurant from 6:30 a.m. until 5:00 p.m., Monday through Saturday. Dinner at John Cross Tavern is served from 5:00 p.m. until 10:00 p.m., Monday through Saturday. The lounge is open until midnight. For reservations (preferred) call (803) 524–3993.

JOHN CROSS TAVERN'S SEAFOOD ST. HELENA

6 tablespoons butter
6 tablespoons flour
3 cups milk
1 tablespoon sherry
10 ounces crab claw meat, drained

10 ounces small shrimp, peeled and deveined
1 cup grated Cheddar cheese
4 slices toasted bread

Melt butter in a saucepan over medium heat. Add flour, stirring until lump-free and blended. Add milk, a little at a time, and stir until mixture thickens. Add sherry and seafood. Stir until well mixed. Pour mixture into an oven-proof dish and sprinkle cheese over top. Broil until cheese starts to brown. Serve seafood with toast. Serves 4.

JOHN CROSS TAVERN'S
LOBSTER AND SHRIMP CREAM SAUCE

3 tablespoons butter
3 tablespoons flour
½ teaspoon onion salt
1½ cups milk

1 cup grated Cheddar
  cheese
sherry to taste
½ cup lobster meat
½ cup shrimp

Melt butter in a saucepan. Stir in flour and onion salt. Add milk and cook over medium to low heat, stirring until mixture thickens. Add cheese and sherry; stir until blended. Add raw seafood, and cook until thoroughly warmed. Pour over 4-ounce servings of your favorite broiled fish. (It's delicious on dolphin or swordfish.) Serves 2 generously.

JOHN CROSS TAVERN'S BLOODY MARY

1½ ounces vodka
½ ounce lemon juice
2 dashes salt
2 dashes pepper

½ ounce Worcestershire
  sauce
½ ounce hot pepper sauce
2 dashes celery salt
4 ounces tomato juice

Pour all ingredients into a shaker container and shake until well blended. Pour over ice in a 10-ounce frosted glass. Serves 1.

THE TURTLE DELI
Summerville

THE TURTLE DELI   The Turtle Deli, as its menu states, is definitely worth the search it takes to find it. It's near the center of town, sandwiched between two local craft shops in a building dating back to the late 1800s. Originally used as a general store, the structure burned to the ground a few years after construction. It was completely rebuilt in 1900 and served the community of Summerville as a variety store and meat market until 1957. It was then condemned and neglected for twenty years until Bob Porter, a local resident with an interest in preservation, began the process of renovation in 1977.

The Turtle Deli, formerly known as The Velvet Turtle, is not your common delicatessen. This cozy restaurant exudes country charm, from the blue-checked tablecloths to the intimate loft area where a portrait of the Marquis de Sade hangs. Wherever you sit, something of interest will catch your eye. On the walls are the Low Country scenes of renowned watercolorist Ravenel Gaillard, who makes his home in the area. A collection of miniature turtles has been donated by many regular customers who, like the restaurant's namesake, prefer the unhurried atmosphere that exists here.

If you arrive at The Turtle Deli during the warm months, you may prefer to dine alfresco in the courtyard. Giant trees provide a natural canopy in this private garden, where bamboo plants and flowering shrubs create an attractive setting.

The menu is devoted exclusively to luncheon fare and features many familiar deli selections, including hot and cold sandwiches, salads and a few specialty items. Quiche is a favorite, and it is delicious. Rita Corbett, the vivacious proprietor and an actress in local little theater productions, knows the woes of the dieter. She recommends the Tuna Salad, which is served over a garden salad with special low-calorie dressing, or you can try a cup of tasty Garden Vegetable Soup.

When it comes to dessert, however, no calories are spared. The popular Cheesecake is thick and creamy, and I doubt you'd be able to stop with one bite. The Chocolate Mocha Cake is also divine.

The Turtle Deli is located at 131 Central Avenue in Summerville. Lunch is served from 10:00 a.m. until 3:00 p.m., Monday through Saturday. Reservations are unnecessary. The telephone number is (803) 875–0380.

THE TURTLE DELI'S BROCCOLI HAM QUICHE

1 unbaked, 9-inch, deep
  dish pie crust
1½ cups grated Swiss
  cheese

1 cup fresh or frozen
  chopped broccoli
¼ pound chopped ham
5 eggs
1 cup half and half

Prick the pie shell, and cover the bottom with Swiss cheese. Top the cheese with broccoli and ham. In a small bowl, beat the eggs and half and half with a wire whisk. Pour over the ingredients in the pie shell. Bake in 350-degree oven for 1 hour and 20 minutes. Yields 1 pie.

THE TURTLE DELI'S CHEESECAKE

1½ sticks margarine
2 cups graham cracker
  crumbs
1¾ cups sugar
2 8-ounce packages cream
  cheese, softened

⅓ cup cornstarch
16 ounces cottage cheese
4 eggs
3 tablespoons lemon juice
2 cups sour cream

Melt ½ stick of the margarine. Mix together graham cracker crumbs, ¼ cup of sugar and the melted margarine. Pat into the bottom of a 10-inch springform pan and set aside. In a large bowl, blend cream cheese, remaining sugar and cornstarch, beating with an electric mixer until thoroughly blended. Put cottage cheese, eggs and lemon juice in a blender con-

79

tainer. Blend on medium speed until well mixed. Pour into the cream cheese mixture and beat well with an electric mixer, about 2 minutes or until thoroughly blended. Melt the remaining stick of margarine and add to the mixture, beating well. Add sour cream and beat until blended. Pour into graham cracker crust. Bake at 350 degrees for 1½ hours. Turn off the oven and leave the cake in the oven for 2 hours. Remove the cheesecake from the oven and allow it to remain at room temperature for an additional 2 hours before serving or refrigerating. Yields 1 cake.

THE TURTLE DELI'S GARDEN VEGETABLE SOUP

3 quarts water
10 beef bouillon cubes
1 16-ounce can diced
　tomatoes
1 pound carrots, sliced

2 large onions, chopped or
　sliced
2 stalks celery, chopped
1 cup corn
1 cup chopped okra
pepper to taste

Add all ingredients to a large soup pot. Bring to a boil, then turn down heat and simmer for at least three hours. Serves 8.

THE JASMINE HOUSE
Eutawville

THE JASMINE HOUSE

I arrived at The Jasmine House in early April, when mother nature casts her magic spell on the South Carolina landscape. Azaleas and camellias were blossoming everywhere. I was pleased to find springtime also in evidence inside the restaurant, where bright fuchsia-colored azalea sprigs nestled in glass goblets at each table, creating a romantic atmosphere in the spacious dining rooms.

The historic building was a popular hotel during the late 1800s. Traveling salesmen, known as "drummers," found the location an ideal place to stay as they peddled their wares at nearby plantations along the Santee River. The structure continued to house paying guests until the 1940s, when it became a private residence.

Restoration of the 1890 building began in 1980, and in early 1981, The Jasmine House opened its doors to the public. The gracious old home once again has become a favorite stop for travelers, who come to enjoy the nearby Santee-Cooper lakes.

The restaurant is named after South Carolina's state flower, the jasmine, and is painted the cheerful yellow color of the flower. The sparkling white terraces and Victorian gingerbread trim add a striking contrast. A wooden porch swing sets the mood for a leisurely visit inside, where you will find a small gift shop.

The Jasmine House menu offers a selection of Low Country items. For lunch, variety is the order of the kitchen, where the menu changes daily. For dinner, appetizers include such favorites as Shrimp and Oyster Cocktails, Oyster Stew and Vegetable Soup. Entrées include seafood platters of Fried Oysters, Deviled Crab and Shrimp. Other dinner listings include charbroiled steaks and various pork and chicken dishes.

Chicken Pie was one of the featured items the afternoon I dined at The Jasmine House. My dining companion and I decided we had, indeed, arrived on the right day because this delicious version of a familiar dish was unlike any we have tasted. No vegetables appeared in the pie. Instead, the tender pieces of chicken, chopped hard-boiled egg and flaky pastry crust provided the main ingredients of this perfectly seasoned dish. A hearty casserole, called Squash Medley, and broccoli spears were tasty accompaniments. And we found the Angel Biscuits impossible to resist.

Dessert proved to be another item I found difficult to refuse, and I was glad when the Grasshopper Pie arrived. My friend was just as pleased with The Jasmine House Mud Pie, which we learned is the favorite with regular customers.

Because I still had a long drive ahead, I declined when wine and beer were offered. I was amused to discover the reason stronger spirits are not available at The Jasmine House. It seems that the restaurant is situated a mere thirty feet short of the required distance from the church across the street to allow for a liquor license. Certain customers have reportedly proposed that the church be moved in order to correct the problem. Most customers, however, seem to find the selections on the wine list sufficiently "spirited" dining accompaniments.

The Jasmine House is located at the corner of Porcher and Gaillard Streets in Eutawville. Lunch is served from 11:30 a.m. until 2:30 p.m., Thursday, Friday and Sunday. Dinner is served from 6:00 p.m. until 9:30 p.m., Thursday, Friday and Saturday. For reservations (recommended for large parties) call (803) 492-3780.

THE JASMINE HOUSE'S ANGEL BISCUITS

1 ¼-ounce package dry
   yeast
2 tablespoons warm water
2½ cups self-rising flour

½ teaspoon baking soda
¼ cup sugar
½ cup vegetable shortening
¾ cup buttermilk

Dissolve yeast in water and set aside. Add flour, baking soda and sugar in a bowl, mixing well. Cut in shortening. Add buttermilk to the yeast mixture, and stir that into the flour mixture until thoroughly blended. Cover and let rise for 90 minutes. Roll dough out onto floured surface and cut it with biscuit cutter. Bake at 350 degrees for 12 to 15 minutes, or until golden brown. Yields 2 dozen biscuits.

THE JASMINE HOUSE'S SQUASH MEDLEY

2 yellow squash
1 zucchini
1 butternut squash (or any
   white squash)
¼ cup chopped onions
salt and pepper to taste

¼ cup cracker crumbs
1 cup grated sharp Cheddar
   cheese
1 egg
⅓ cup milk

Clean all squash and slice diagonally. Combine squash with onions, and add to one cup boiling water. Salt and pepper to taste. Cook until tender, approximately 5 minutes. Drain the squash and onions and mix with crumbs and cheese. Combine egg with milk in a small bowl, beating until well blended. Add to squash mixture. Turn into greased casserole, and bake at 400 degrees for 35 minutes until mixture is set and lightly browned. Serves 4.

THE JASMINE HOUSE'S CHICKEN PIE

1 2- to 3-pound stewing
   hen, cooked
¼ cup chopped onions
1 large hard-boiled egg,
   chopped

1 cup chicken stock
salt and pepper to taste
¼ cup shortening
1 cup all-purpose flour
¼ cup cold water

Pull chicken from bones and combine it with onions, egg, chicken stock, salt and pepper. Pour into a baking dish and set aside. Cut shortening into flour, blending with water. Roll dough out on a floured board into a circle large enough to fit over the casserole. Cover chicken mixture loosely with pastry. Bake at 350 degrees until golden brown, about 35 minutes. Serves 6.

McPHERSON'S DRY DOCK
Denmark

McPHERSON'S DRY DOCK

For a house that once sat on the wrong side of the tracks, the structure known today as McPherson's Dry Dock has literally come a long way.

When the arrival of railroads crisscrossing through Denmark made the homesite of the Fred McCrae family noisy, they knew it was time to move. The family dismantled their beloved pine cottage, which dates back to the early 1900s, and had it moved to its present double corner lot near downtown. Many of Julia McCrae's former students still stop by to visit their late teacher's home. Most of the students and friends are pleased at how carefully William McPherson and Mike Booth have transformed the historic house into a restaurant.

During remodeling, it was discovered that the home was the second house built in Denmark. A few interesting antique treasures were found, such as the 1864 Indian penny that was uncovered in an upstairs fireplace.

Also during remodeling, the owners decided to add the long wooden entry ramp that now winds up to the restaurant's broad porch. The ramp, which is located next to a concrete stairway, is a welcome aid to those whose choice of restaurants is limited by physical handicaps.

You will be pleased with the inviting and casual atmosphere that waits inside McPherson's Dry Dock. The former parlor wins my vote for the most attractive dining room in the home. The soft blue walls contrast handsomely with the white fireplace and wood trim. Almost all of the windows contain the original glass panes, and the paneled doors and porcelain door knobs are the same ones used by the McCraes.

Surely the McCrae offspring would approve of the Dry Dock's menu, which advertises seafood for landlubbers. You will find many platter-sized servings of breaded and broiled seafood items to please even the hungriest mate. And for the ones in the group who prefer something other than fish, there is always Southern Fried Chicken or the old standby, Hamburger and Fries.

I had been told that the Catfish Stew enjoys such popularity that the owners are considering marketing the item. After only a few spoonfuls of the hearty, sweet soup, the reason was apparent. After polishing off the stew and nibbling on the Hushpuppies, the Green Shrimp Salad turned out to be almost too filling, but I managed to make room. If you can even think about dessert after your meal, a perfect choice might be the Pecan or Lemon Pie.

Children under the age of six are guests of the house, and special rates apply to children under twelve and to senior citizens. It was apparent from the many families present the night I dined here that this, indeed, is a place to bring the whole clan.

The Dry Dock is located on the corner of Maple Street and East Coker in Denmark. Lunch is served from 11:00 a.m. until 2:00 p.m. on Friday. Dinner is served from 5:00 p.m. until 10:00 p.m., Tuesday through Saturday. Reservations are unnecessary, but the telephone number is (803) 793–4364.

McPHERSON'S DRY DOCK'S GREEN SHRIMP SALAD

10 ounces medium shrimp,
   peeled and deveined
2 cups shredded lettuce
1 tomato, quartered

1 lemon, quartered
½ cup sliced peaches
½ cup sliced cucumbers
2 to 3 apple rings

Add shrimp to boiling water and boil until pink, about 2 minutes. Drain shrimp and chill. Arrange lettuce on two serving plates, leaving an opening in the center of each. Fill the openings with shrimp and surround with remaining ingredients in an attractive manner. Serves 2.

McPHERSON'S DRY DOCK'S OYSTER STEW

1 tablespoon butter
12 select oysters
1¼ cups whole milk

salt and pepper to taste
dash Tabasco sauce to taste

Melt butter in a saucepan. Add oysters and sauté for 2 to 3 minutes. Add remaining ingredients and cook over medium heat until hot. Serve immediately. Serves 2.

McPHERSON'S DRY DOCK'S COCKTAIL SAUCE

1 cup catsup   **salt and pepper to taste**
1 teaspoon horseradish   **Tabasco sauce to taste**

In a small bowl, mix all ingredients until flavors are well blended. Serve with seafood. Yields 1 cup.

ARTHUR'S ON MAIN
Sumter

ARTHUR'S ON MAIN My initial impression of Arthur's on Main was, I'm afraid, mistaken. The sight of a white mansion, with its impressive facade of Ionic columns, made me expect a formal, stuffy atmosphere. But, as we sometimes discover, first impressions do not last long.

What I found inside was lighthearted elegance. Formal antiques, such as the lead crystal chandelier in the entrance hall, create a delightful contrast to the collection of leafy plants that thrive in claw-footed bathtubs. Whimsical contradictions like these appear throughout the restaurant, making it anything but stuffy.

The credit for the mansion's tasteful décor must be given to the owner and manager, Arthur Gose, Jr., after whom the restaurant is named. His appreciation for historic structures and elegant dining prompted him to restore the former residence, which was built in the mid-1800s for the Alfred Scarborough family.

Each of the indoor dining rooms is distinctive in décor. Even the front and back porches are put to attractive and practical use when weather permits, and alfresco dining has become a favorite at Arthur's. The wide front veranda is the place many summertime guests prefer to dine, especially when one of the Little Theater productions is performed there. For those who enjoy a more intimate outdoor setting, there is a gazebo area on the back porch.

By now you should know that there isn't a bad seat in the house. You can expect the cuisine to be just as diverse as the seating. The menu changes frequently to avoid the dullness that Arthur considers unforgivable. However, such all-time favorites as Scampi or Prime Rib are offered year-round.

For dinner, I put my appetite in Arthur's hands, and he assured me that I wouldn't be disappointed. He is a man who speaks the truth; the dishes that arrived at my table were the proof. First came the chilled glass of Canteval rosé, followed by a plate of Stuffed Mushrooms covered with a creamy cheese sauce. My entrée of fork-tender Prime Rib of

Beef au Jus was accompanied by hot horseradish sauce. Now I know why the restaurant's regular patrons insist that this dish remain on the menu.

The dessert menu had so many luscious-sounding confections that I couldn't decide between them. Arthur came to the rescue again with a suggestion that I try a liquid dessert. How could I resist a drink with a name like Heart Throb? This frothy delight was a perfect way to top off the evening.

Lunch is served at Arthur's, too, with a menu that ranges from lasagna to quiches, salads and sandwiches. If you arrive on a Saturday, plan to order from a brunch menu that salutes the weekend with champagne and some very special omelets.

Arthur's on Main is located at 425 North Main Street in Sumter. Lunch is served from 11:00 a.m. until 2:00 p.m., Tuesday through Saturday. Dinner is served from 5:00 p.m. until 10:00 p.m., Tuesday through Saturday. For reservations (recommended) call (803) 775–1776.

ARTHUR'S ON MAIN'S STUFFED MUSHROOMS

2 tablespoons butter
½ cup finely chopped
  mushroom stems
½ cup finely chopped ham
½ cup Parmesan cheese
2 tablespoons parsley flakes

¼ cup bread crumbs
¼ cup flour
¼ cup half and half
16 large mushroom caps
fresh parsley for garnish

Melt butter in a large skillet, and sauté mushroom stems until tender. Remove and set aside. Add ham, cheese and parsley flakes to butter remaining in skillet and sauté, mixing well. In a separate bowl, mix bread crumbs and flour with a fork until well blended. Add crumbs to the skillet and stir into the ham and cheese mixture. Add mushroom stems and half and half, stirring until mixture is thick. Remove from heat. Stuff each mushroom cap with 1 teaspoon of mixture. Top all with Cheese Sauce (recipe follows) and garnish with fresh parsley. Serves 4.

Cheese Sauce:

2 tablespoons butter	¼ cup water
2 tablespoons flour	½ cup grated American or
1 cup half and half	Cheddar cheese

Melt butter in a saucepan and add flour, stirring until smooth. Gradually add half and half and water; stir until mixture comes to a boil. Reduce heat, add cheese and stir until well blended. Pour cheese sauce over mushrooms and bake, covered, in a 375-degree oven until hot and bubbling, about 10 minutes.

ARTHUR'S ON MAIN'S CREAM OF ZUCCHINI SOUP

6 large zucchini	½ teaspoon black pepper
1 cup chicken broth	½ teaspoon white pepper
cold water	1 teaspoon freeze-dried
1 teaspoon salt	chives
½ teaspoon onion salt	1 cup half and half

Peel the zucchini and slice diagonally. Place it in a soup pot and add broth and enough cold water to cover. Bring to a boil, and cook until tender. Reserve liquid. Remove zucchini and purée in electric blender. Return to chicken broth and add all the remaining ingredients except half and half. Cook over medium heat until warmed through. Add half and half, and stir the soup until heated, but do not boil. Makes 4 to 6 servings.

ARTHUR'S ON MAIN'S HEART THROB

1½ ounces Midori	dash Grenadine
1½ ounces vodka	3 ice cubes
2 ounces orange juice	

Combine all ingredients in a blender container. Blend on high speed until frothy. Serves 1.

THE NEWTON HOUSE
Bennettsville

THE NEWTON HOUSE

I can't tell you how good the mug of piping hot Broccoli Chowder tasted on the cold and windy day I visited The Newton House. The soup was but one reason the chill disappeared so quickly from my shivering bones. Although it was dreary and gray outdoors, I felt as though the sun was shining inside this unique restaurant. The walls in the front dining room are painted the brightest shade of yellow imaginable. You will discover, as I did, that a visit to this restaurant is an introduction to color as you've never seen it before. And it begins before you open the front door.

The exterior of the stately Victorian home, located near downtown Bennettsville, is painted an eye-catching Williamsburg blue. Inside, on both levels of the restaurant, walls are painted shocking shades of poppy red, royal blue, kelly green and cocoa brown.

Co-owner Julia Ballou gives the credit for the exciting décor to her partner and son-in-law, Stephen Smith, whose theatrical background may be responsible for the many clever ideas used throughout the house. It was his idea to use the original closet doors as attractive tabletops. Other creative touches include produce crates and baskets that hang from the ceiling and the back-to-back fireplaces that separate the upstairs bar and lounge from the dining area.

Built in 1905 for the Smith Newton family, this two-story house remained in the family until 1979, when it was sold and converted into this charming restaurant. Mrs. Ballou saw no need to change the name of the structure after the purchase. "This place had been called The Newton House for over seventy-five years, and a new name wouldn't change a thing."

Structurally, little has changed during the transformation from residence to restaurant. Solid posts that measure four feet square run from the basement to the attic. All fireplaces are original and in working order, as is the kitchen where Mrs. Ballou's Yankee recipes are prepared to the delight of her Southern customers.

Creativity does not stop with the décor, as the menu attests.

Luncheon offerings appear on a mini-newspaper, and the evening's appetizer and dinner menus are presented on wine bottles.

I've already raved about the Broccoli Chowder. Another item I found irresistible is their delicious bread, creatively served in a small crock. Let others rave about The Newton House's Veal Parmigiana and New York Strip. My vote goes to their succulent Chicken Diane, which owes its appeal to the unique combination of brandy-mustard sauce. The perfect enhancement for my taste buds was a chilled glass of smooth chardonnay that provided all the dessert my figure could afford.

The Newton House is located at 205 McColl Street in Bennettsville. Lunch is served from 11:30 a.m. until 2:00 p.m., Monday through Friday. Dinner is served from 6:00 p.m. until 9:30 p.m., Tuesday through Saturday. For reservations (recommended) call (803) 479–2272.

THE NEWTON HOUSE'S CHICKEN DIANE

4 boneless chicken breasts
dash salt and pepper
3 tablespoons olive oil
3 tablespoons butter
4 tablespoons chopped
  onions
½ teaspoon garlic powder

2 tablespoons chopped
  fresh parsley
2 tablespoons brandy
2 teaspoons Dijon mustard
1 teaspoon Worcestershire
  sauce
4 tablespoons chicken broth

Leave skin on the chicken breasts, and flatten with a mallet. Salt and pepper both sides of breasts, and set aside. Melt olive oil and butter in a skillet. Add chicken breasts and brown, skin side first. Cook until done. Remove chicken and keep it warm in the oven. Add onions, garlic powder and parsley to the skillet, and sauté for one minute. Add brandy and scrape pan. Lower heat and add mustard, Worcestershire sauce and chicken broth. Mix quickly and serve on top of chicken. Serves 4.

THE NEWTON HOUSE'S BROCCOLI CHOWDER

1 large bunch fresh broccoli
4 cups chicken broth
¾ cup half and half

2 cups milk
1 cup grated Swiss cheese
salt and pepper to taste

Trim tough outer covering from broccoli stalks. Cut with a medium blade in a food processor until all stalks are chopped. In a soup pot, simmer broccoli stalks and florets in chicken broth until tender. Add remaining ingredients and heat slowly over low heat. Do not boil. Serves 6.

THE NEWTON HOUSE'S VINAIGRETTE DRESSING

1 cup salad oil
⅓ cup apple cider vinegar
1 tablespoon lemon juice
1½ teaspoons Dijon
  mustard

½ teaspoon coarse, ground
  black pepper
salt to taste

Combine all ingredients in a bowl. Whip with whisk until well blended. Shake well before serving. Yields 1½ cups.

THE PADDOCK
Camden

THE PADDOCK

How many people do you know who have been given last rites three times in the same day and lived to tell the story? This is one story among many that retired steeplechase jockey Nick Butler told me while I was dining in his posh, tavern-style restaurant. The rites were administered to the protesting Irishman after a nearly fatal jump in his native Ireland. An accident like that might persuade most people to pursue another occupation, but as one of Nick's trainers remarked, "You can tell he's Irish, but you can't tell him much."

Butler went on to have several more accidents and earn racing fame in this country before deciding to open a French restaurant in Camden. He named it The Paddock, an especially apt name for a restaurant in an equestrian community that plays hosts to two international steeplechase events. Even the "regulars" can barely squeeze into The Paddock during Camden's spring Carolina Cup or the fall Colonial Cup.

My daughter and I visited The Paddock on a warm summer Friday. Looking forward to the weekend, I indulged in a Bloody Mary as Daintry and I sat in the dining room listening to Nick's entertaining stories. Seated on burgundy velvet Louis XIV chairs, we admired the restaurant's brick Roman arches and the original 1866 prints from Nick's grandmother's estate in County Meath, Ireland.

For lunch, we left the formal white tablecloths to dine in the casual bar. Pianist Betty Blackwell, who had been playing old favorites, joined us for lunch. She suggested the Paddock Burger, served with bacon on an English muffin, for Daintry. The burger is a departure from such French dishes as my creamy Seafood Crepe, prepared al dente in order not to mask the integrity of the crabmeat, which was served with cauliflower and hollandaise sauce.

Nick prepares the evening meal himself. The bite of Breast of Chicken a l'Orange that I sampled was luscious. I also can heartily recommend the Veal Francais, an easily prepared and delicious entrée. Dessert had to be shared because neither of us alone could have finished the generous portion of their wonderful Hot Apples with Ice Cream.

It might be true—you might not be able to tell an Irishman much—but someone certainly told this one how to cook.

The Paddock is located at 514 Rutledge Street in Camden. Lunch is served from 11:30 a.m. until 2:00 p.m., Tuesday through Saturday. Dinner is served from 6:00 p.m. until 10:30 p.m, Tuesday through Saturday. The bar serves from 5:00 p.m. until 2:00 a.m, Tuesday through Saturday. For reservations call (803) 432–3222.

THE PADDOCK'S BREAST OF CHICKEN A L'ORANGE

4 boneless chicken breasts   **3 to 4 tablespoons butter**
¾ cup flour   **wild rice (follow package**
salt and pepper to taste   **directions)**

Dredge the chicken breasts in flour that has been seasoned with salt and pepper. Place butter in a skillet over high heat. When the butter melts, add the chicken and brown quickly on both sides until golden brown. Reduce heat to medium-low and cook the chicken for 25 to 40 minutes. (It should be done, but still tender.)

Orange Sauce:
1 tablespoon cornstarch   **½ cup sugar**
¼ cup water   **2 tablespoons curacao**
2 cups orange juice   **liqueur**
1 teaspoon cider vinegar

Combine cornstarch with water in a cup and stir until dissolved. Combine orange juice, vinegar and sugar in a saucepan over medium-high heat. Stir until sugar is dissolved. Add cornstarch mixture and stir until sauce boils and thickens. Add curacao and stir until all flavors are combined. Place the chicken on a bed of cooked wild rice and ladle sauce generously over top. Serves 4.

THE PADDOCK'S VEAL FRANCAIS

2 4-ounce escallops of veal
6 tablespoons butter
½ cup quartered fresh
  mushrooms

½ cup flour, plus 2
  tablespoons
salt and pepper to taste
⅓ cup Madeira wine

Pound the veal with a meat mallet until thin; set aside. Place 4 tablespoons of butter in a saucepan and sauté mushrooms for 2 to 3 minutes; set aside in a warm place. Season ½ cup of flour with salt and pepper and dredge the veal. Place veal in the saucepan and sauté both sides, about 1 minute each. (Do not overcook.) Remove and keep warm with mushrooms. Add the 2 tablespoons of butter to the saucepan with remaining 2 tablespoons of flour. Stir until smooth. Add the wine, and immediately ignite the sauce with a match. Allow the flame to extinguish itself, then stir the sauce. Place the veal on two plates, and add mushrooms and a healthy dollop of sauce to each serving. Serves 2.

THE PADDOCK'S HOT APPLES AND ICE CREAM

1 20-ounce can of chopped
  apples
¾ cup sugar
¼ teaspoon salt
1 teaspoon cinnamon

½ teaspoon nutmeg
2 tablespoons butter
4 large scoops vanilla ice
  cream
1 cup whipped cream

To a medium saucepan add apples, sugar, salt, cinnamon, nutmeg and butter. Cook over medium heat until the butter melts, then lower the heat to a simmer. Stir the mixture and cook approximately 15 to 20 minutes. To serve, put a scoop of ice cream into a brandy snifter or goblet. Ladle a generous amount of hot apple mixture over the ice cream and top with whipped cream. Serves 4.

THE CAPITOL RESTAURANT
Columbia

THE CAPITOL RESTAURANT

According to local Columbia lore, a certain young man seeking a circuit judgeship was informed that, if he truly wanted to be elected, he should first "score points at the cafe." The cafe with such a powerful reputation is none other than the unpretentious black and white restaurant on Main Street.

Although the cafe is only a half-block walk from the State Capitol, it doesn't seem the type of place that can make or break reputations. Perhaps that's because the restaurant's interior is humble and has remained virtually unchanged since the place opened for business in 1905. The stools still swivel under the wooden counter, while old-fashioned furnaces stand at both ends of the one-room cafe. Behind the counter are some faded photos taken after the Civil War. If you take the time to look at them, you'll be stunned by the destruction suffered by Columbia during those violent years.

No one pays attention to the fact that this place is actually The Capitol Restaurant. The name printed on the menu as well as on the National Register reads "Capitol Cafe." To the regulars, it is simply "the cafe."

The cafe has become known as a haven for those who are hungry for good home cooking. This restaurant caters to an interesting and unusual clientele. Legislators, government officials and mill workers can be found rubbing elbows at the counter, along with the University of South Carolina students who live in the dormitories across the street. The restaurant's twenty-four-hour schedule appeals to those who work the late shift, cram for exams or suffer from insomnia.

Current owner John Foster continues to serve the dishes that the former proprietor, Amelia Siokis, introduced during her fifty-year reign at the cafe. You occasionally can find Mrs. Siokis mingling with guests, some of whom are the grand-children of her former customers.

As might be expected at a restaurant that never closes, you will find a menu listing everything from breakfast fare to midnight snacks. Other reasons for this restaurant's popularity

102

are its economical prices and hearty servings. I can imagine how much college students appreciate the over-sized portions of Spaghetti with Meatballs and the bountiful Seafood Platter. A specialty of the house is the Greek Salad, a hand-me-down recipe from Mrs. Siokis. I sampled a bit of the tasty salad and a hearty Ham and Cheese Omelet that has become a favorite with night owls and students.

Watching the flow of restaurant regulars is a show in itself, but you may want to schedule your visit to the cafe on a Tuesday night when the unnamed bluegrass band performs. On this special night, you may be able to catch the antics of some otherwise conservative legislator joining in the hootenanny with the late night crew from the mill. It doesn't take long to understand that it's not important that the décor is not ultra chic and the cuisine less than cordon bleu. As one knowledgeable source put it: "This is simply one of the most prestigious men's clubs in town, and it costs not a penny to join."

The Capitol Restaurant is located at 1210 Main Street in Columbia. Meals are served twenty-four hours a day. Reservations are not accepted, but the phone number is (803) 765–0176.

THE CAPITOL RESTAURANT'S GREEK SALAD

1 head iceberg lettuce
2 stalks celery, diced
1 medium onion, diced
3 tomatoes, diced
2 cups crumbled feta cheese

1 2-ounce can anchovies
4 teaspoons basil
1 cup commercial oil and
   vinegar dressing

In a large salad bowl, break lettuce into bite-size pieces. Add celery, onion and tomatoes. Add cheese and lay anchovies over top. Sprinkle basil over all ingredients. Pour oil and vinegar dressing over salad before serving. Serves 6.

THE CAPITOL RESTAURANT'S SPAGHETTI SAUCE

1 pound ground sirloin
2 tablespoons olive oil
½ garlic clove, minced
½ cup minced celery
½ cup minced onions
2½ cups tomato juice
1 6-ounce can tomato paste

½ teaspoon basil
½ teaspoon thyme
½ teaspoon oregano
¼ teaspoon salt
2 cups beef broth
1 pound spaghetti

Brown the sirloin in olive oil; drain well. In a large saucepan, combine meat with all the remaining ingredients except the spaghetti. Stir well and simmer for 2 to 3 hours until the flavors are well blended and the sauce is thick. Cook spaghetti noodles according to package directions. Pour sauce over the noodles. Serves 4 to 6.

THE CAPITOL RESTAURANT'S
HAM AND CHEESE OMELET

1 tablespoon oil
2 eggs
¼ cup grated Cheddar
  cheese

¼ cup diced ham
salt and pepper to taste

Heat oil in a skillet. Beat the eggs and pour into the skillet. Sprinkle cheese and ham pieces over the eggs, and cook for one minute. Fold one side over the other; cook until eggs are lightly browned. Salt and pepper to taste. Serves 1.

THE LOADING DOCK
Columbia

THE LOADING DOCK If you had visited the building now known as The Loading Dock in the early 1900s, you would not have found a restaurant and bar complex serving tempting food for the body. Instead, you would have found a warehouse containing food for the mind.

This historic structure, built in 1913, originally was designed as a book depository for the state public school system. No expense seems to have been spared during its construction if we are to judge by what remains today. The sturdy evidence is found in the solid brick exterior walls measuring thirteen inches thick and in the elaborate sprinkler system installed in 1923.

The fire protection system must have been quite elaborate for its day because it continues to serve as the building's primary extinguishing system. You'll find the fire protection equipment artistically displayed in The Saloon on the first floor.

Also blending beautifully with the building's eclectic décor is the original book scale near the entrance. English antiques and American mementos are scattered throughout the two-level restaurant and bar complex. On the first floor, which contains The Saloon and The Oyster Bar, are such stunning pieces as stained-glass panels, mahogany bars, inlaid marble counter tops and a player piano.

The Upper Deck on the second level is reserved for dining and contains its own complete bar. A mingling of old and new can be found on The Upper Deck's menu. The management tells me it is basically American, but I found some continental entrées, along with a few unusual dishes.

One look at the appetizer menu and I knew I would have to try the Hot Mozzarella Sticks and flash-fried Artichoke Hearts. Each of these delightful items is served with its own special sauce. What a way to begin a meal.

Still in the mood for the unusual, I ordered the Marinated Chicken for my luncheon entrée. The sweet-and-sour tender breast of chicken was so good I asked for the recipe. This popular offering also appears on the evening menu.

Completely ignoring the fact that I had finished everything on all plates placed before me, I went ahead and ordered dessert. How can you resist ice cream in flavors called Snickers, Reese's Peanut Butter or Grand Marnier? I went with the chocolate and peanut butter combination, and the only thing I can say is it's worth every calorie.

The dinner menu aims to please any palate, whether the preference is for steak, seafood or chicken, or you can mix and match a combination platter.

If you're in the mood for a nightcap, you may stay right where you are and have an after-dinner drink whipped up in the bar and brought to your table. Or, if you would like to join the throng waiting to get into Julian's, there is a private stairway leading from the dining room to The Loading Dock's new high-tech night club.

The Loading Dock is located at 1310 Gadsden Street in Columbia. Lunch is served from 11:30 a.m. until 2:30 p.m., Monday through Friday. Dinner is served from 5:30 p.m. until 10:30 p.m., Monday through Saturday. For reservations (recommended) call (803) 256–2741.

THE LOADING DOCK'S
CREAM OF MUSHROOM SOUP

3 tablespoons butter
1 medium onion, diced
2 stalks celery, minced
¾ pound fresh mushrooms, sliced
3 tablespoons sifted all-purpose flour

2 cups chilled beef stock or broth
2 cups half and half
¼ teaspoon nutmeg
dash white pepper
salt to taste
½ teaspoon chervil (optional)

Melt butter in a large sauté pan over medium heat. Add onions and celery. Sauté until vegetables are soft but not brown. Add sliced mushrooms and continue cooking until mushrooms are soft. Sprinkle flour over mixture, stirring constantly. Add stock, stirring vigorously. As soon as stock

107

has been incorporated, add half and half; stir until smooth. Bring soup almost to a boil and reduce heat. Add seasonings and simmer for 10 minutes, stirring occasionally. Serves 4.

THE LOADING DOCK'S MARINATED CHICKEN

3 cups canned pineapple
juice
1 cup dry sherry
1 cup sugar
½ teaspoon ground ginger

¼ cup soy sauce
1 cup orange juice
1 3- to 4-pound frying
chicken, cut up

Mix the first six ingredients in a bowl, stirring until the sugar is thoroughly dissolved. Pour marinade over chicken, making sure all pieces are covered. Refrigerate for a minimum of 24 hours. Chicken may be broiled, barbecued, baked or braised. Baste with marinade several times while chicken cooks. After using, discard marinade. Serves 4.

THE LOADING DOCK'S SEAFOOD GUMBO

½ stick butter
2 tablespoons flour
1 quart water
6 medium tomatoes, peeled
and seeded
1½ pounds fresh okra,
sliced
1 pound fresh raw shrimp

½ dozen raw oysters
½ pound fresh crabmeat
1 pound fresh flounder or
turbot
2 cups canned clams
salt and pepper to taste
gumbo file powder to taste
4 cups cooked rice

Melt butter in a soup pot and add flour, stirring constantly until a smooth, brown roux has been achieved. Add water, tomatoes and okra. Reduce heat to low and cook slowly for one hour. Add seafood and cook on medium heat for 15 minutes. Add seasonings and blend into mixture. Serve over cooked rice in individual serving bowls. Serves 4 to 6.

VILLA TRONCO RISTORANTE
Columbia

VILLA TRONCO
RISTORANTE

"It's called pizza. Try it, you'll like it." Nobody would order this unknown item forty years ago, so Sadie Tronco literally had to give it away. Word spread, and before long Sadie was inundated with local customers and throngs of homesick Italian soldiers from nearby Fort Jackson. Needless to say, these soldiers were hungry for authentic Italian cooking. Such enthusiasm ensured the survival of Italian cuisine in Columbia and made a place for three generations of the Tronco family, including Sadie herself, who is now in her eighties.

The restaurant's beginnings can be traced back to the early 1940s, but the building housing the restaurant dates back to the mid-1800s, when it was built for the Palmetto Fire Engine Company. Reportedly, it is the only remaining nineteenth-century firehouse in the Midland area of South Carolina. Exterior restoration took place in the summer of 1983. Layers of stucco were removed, uncovering the original brick facade. The granite plaque revealing the name of the fire engine company and its 1858 incorporation date now hangs above the door.

The brick stable, added to the rear of the firehouse in 1903, has been converted to a two-level dining room with a skylight to give an open, airy effect. Take note of the cast-iron fire insurance plaque that hangs near the room divider. This metal plate reminds us of the days when fire protection was a conditional thing—no plaque, no protection.

The dinner menu at Villa Tronco is impressive. All items appear in Italian, with English subtitles underneath. Whenever I think of Italian food, I think of Chianti. So I ordered a selection of the red table wine to complement my meal. My entrée was preceded by a crisp house salad topped with diced cheese and a small loaf of warm fresh bread that tasted as I hoped it would—crusty on the outside and soft and chewy inside. Fortunately, my entrée of Shrimp Fettuccine arrived before I devoured the entire loaf. The plate of green and white fettuccine, tossed with cream, cheese, butter and shrimp, smelled divine and tasted as good as it looked.

I thought I wouldn't have room for dessert, but with Mama Sadie's famous Amaretto Cheesecake staring me in the face, I made room. Mama Mia! The cheesecake was wonderful, as was their special preparation of Caffe Cappuccino.

Another bonus at the Villa Tronco is the variety of take-home items, including cheesecakes and other Tronco specialties. I later shared these purchases with my family, who proclaimed Mama Tronco's cuisine bravissimo!

Villa Tronco Ristorante is located at 1213 Blanding Street in Columbia. Lunch is served from 11:00 a.m. until 3:00 p.m., Monday through Saturday. Dinner is served from 5:00 p.m. until 11:00 p.m. For reservations (recommended) call (803) 256–7677.

VILLA TRONCO RISTORANTE'S
SHRIMP FETTUCCINE

1 stick butter, room temperature	½ cup heavy cream
½ cup grated Parmesan cheese	1 pound fettuccine
	1 pound shrimp, boiled and deveined

In a small bowl, beat butter with a wooden spoon until creamy. Gradually add cheese and cream, beating until fluffy. Cook the fettuccine al dente. Transfer the hot, drained fettuccine onto a warm platter. Add the cream sauce and shrimp, and toss until well mixed. Serves 4.

VILLA TRONCO RISTORANTE'S
CAFFE CAPPUCCINO

3 ounces expresso coffee	dash cinnamon
4 ounces steamed milk	4 ounces whipped cream

Brew the expresso. Pour hot expresso, steamed milk and cinnamon into a tall mug. Stir to blend. Top with whipped cream. Serves 1.

VILLA TRONCO RISTORANTE'S PASTA
WITH WHITE CLAM SAUCE

½ cup olive oil
2 minced cloves garlic
½ cup water
1 teaspoon parsley
½ teaspoon salt

½ teaspoon oregano
½ teaspoon white pepper
2 cups whole clams with
juice
1 pound pasta, cooked

Heat olive oil in a skillet. Add garlic and sauté until light brown in color. Slowly stir in water, parsley, salt, oregano, pepper and clams. Continue cooking over low heat until the clams are heated through. Serve over the cooked pasta. Serves 4.

THE GREENHOUSE RESTAURANT
Aiken

**THE GREENHOUSE
RESTAURANT**

You can enter The Greenhouse Restaurant through the canopied street entrance or from the lobby of the Holley Inn. I suggest the lobby route, because a walk through this grand, old hotel will send you pleasantly back in time to the glittering days of Aiken's Golden Era.

The town of Aiken was celebrating its heyday when B. F. Holley built his luxury hotel in 1929. It was a time when the good life revolved around fox hunts, thoroughbred horse races and polo matches. Years before, Thomas and Louise Hitchcock had found the area ideal for thoroughbred raising and training. This illustrious couple introduced horses to Aiken in the 1870s, causing the area to be known as "Thoroughbred Country." A horse-centered existence is still the way of life for many in this verdant countryside.

Lining the walls of this charming restaurant are framed photographs of the Hitchcocks, dressed in their hunting and riding attire. If you take a close look at these photos, you'll notice they were taken before the advent of color film, when hand painting was done to bring black-and-white subjects to life.

As you might expect from the restaurant's name, the décor centers around plants. Potted palms and other attractive greenery abound in this airy garden setting. You'll even find a miniature palm on each table. Scenes of Casablanca come to mind in this room where shutters block the sun's rays and ceiling fans whir overhead.

We arrived at The Greenhouse in time for lunch. Everything on the menu sounded good. The crock of Onion Soup proved to be a flavorful first course. The chef's salad was a perfect follow-up. Piled high on a lettuce bed were layers of thinly sliced turkey and ham and an assortment of cheeses and garnishes. My luncheon companion ordered the Stuffed Green Peppers and a side plate of Deep Dish Brown Rice, and from the way he tackled these selections, I knew he was pleased with his luncheon, also.

I asked to see the dinner menu, and the Southern Fried

Chicken with Fried Bananas sounded so intriguing that I took the recipe home for testing. If you have never tried bananas prepared this way, you are missing a wonderfully different taste treat.

You also will find such familiar favorites as Filet Mignon and Chicken Cordon Bleu on the dinner menu. The dessert list is tempting, so be ready to choose between the Cheesecake, Strawberry Shortcake and the Parfaits. May all of your decisions be so sweet.

The Greenhouse Restaurant is located in the Holley Inn at 235 Richland West in Aiken. Breakfast and lunch are served daily from 6:30 a.m. until 2:30 p.m. Dinner is served from 6:00 p.m. until 10:00 p.m., Monday through Saturday. For reservations (recommended) call (803) 648–4265.

THE GREENHOUSE RESTAURANT'S
DEEP DISH BROWN RICE

1 cup raw brown rice	1 stick butter, melted
1 10-ounce can beef	¼ teaspoon oregano
consommé	¼ teaspoon lemon-seasoned
1 10-ounce can beef	salt
bouillon	

Place rice in a three-quart casserole dish. Add consommé, bouillon and butter. Stir mixture once. Sprinkle with oregano and lemon salt. Bake, covered, in a 350-degree oven for one hour. If more moisture is needed, sprinkle lightly with water. Serves 4 to 6.

THE GREENHOUSE RESTAURANT'S
FRIED BANANAS

1 banana	1 teaspoon mayonnaise
½ cup self-rising flour	¼ teaspoon cinnamon
1 cup cooking oil or fat	¼ cup finely chopped
¼ cup honey	pecans

Peel the banana and cut lengthwise into four sections. Roll each section in flour. Fry in hot oil until golden brown; drain. Combine honey, mayonnaise and cinnamon, mixing well so flavors are thoroughly blended. Pour honey sauce over bananas and sprinkle with pecans. Serves 1 or 2.

NOTE: This dish is delicious served with fried chicken.

THE GREENHOUSE RESTAURANT'S
STUFFED GREEN PEPPERS

6 large green peppers
1 pound lean ground beef
2 tablespoons chopped
  onions
1 teaspoon salt
⅛ teaspoon garlic salt
1 cup converted rice, cooked
1 15-ounce can tomato sauce
¾ cup grated Mozzarella
  cheese

Cut the top off of each pepper and remove insides. Cook the peppers for five minutes in enough boiling water to cover; remove from water. In skillet, cook ground beef and onions until meat is brown. Drain meat and add salt, garlic salt, rice and one cup of tomato sauce; heat thoroughly. Stuff each pepper with meat mixture. Stand peppers upright in an ungreased baking dish, and pour the remaining tomato sauce over them. Bake, covered, in a 350-degree oven for 45 minutes. Uncover and cook 15 minutes longer. Sprinkle with cheese before serving. Serves 6.

UP YOUR ALLEY
Aiken

UP YOUR ALLEY

Aiken deservedly prides itself in the renovation of the downtown historic area. And, in my opinion, there is no place more eye-catching than Up Your Alley. The proprietors of this lively restaurant have innovatively arranged all stools and tables in the saloon so that guests are always at eye level with each other, whether sitting or standing. Psychologically, it is a great icebreaker.

Don't plan to focus your eyes on any one thing for long, however, because the saloon contains quite a collection of memorabilia. Traffic signs, old posters and various license plates, including one from the Cayman Islands, decorate the saloon. You may want to sit in the authentic barber's chair near the entrance. I chose a quieter seat to try a drink called The Alley Cat. This light and frothy drink includes amaretto, pineapple juice and ice cream, and it seemed a perfect way to begin my visit.

Three young men, each with an eye for detail and a pair of deft hands in the kitchen, have cleverly transformed this historic structure into an inviting series of dining rooms. It's hard to believe that the turn-of-the-century building once was considered an eyesore.

The atmosphere in the dining rooms combines Victorian primness with country comfort. Salvaged treasures from old homes and area churches, such as mahogany benches and stained glass, are attractively used throughout. I was particularly impressed with the music room, which is decorated with instruments, sheet music and photos of old opera stars.

The food at Up Your Alley is every bit as special as the décor. I needed help making a decision and found it when the chef suggested the Fried Artichoke Hearts and Beer Batter Pickles as appetizers. If you have never eaten either of these unusual foods, your taste buds have been living in a state of deprivation.

Since the chef did such a good job with the first course, I left the next one up to him as well. He came through again,

118

because the Avocado Stuffed with Shrimp Salad was a true winner. Other luncheon offerings are such international specialties as Pita Pocket Sandwiches, Mexican Burritos, Fettuccine Alfredo and Crepe a la Reine.

If you have any room left after finishing the hearty entrées, you may want to choose from the dessert list, which includes such favorites as Cheesecake, Fresh Fruit and Baklava. Or, you may want to order one of their special liqueur-laced coffees.

Up Your Alley offers an excellent dinner menu that features continental fare like Chicken Kiev, Veal Jerusalem, Scallops Bar Harbor and Steak au Poivre.

A complete wine list, containing both imported and domestic vintages, is available. The Ulrich Langguth Reisling has become a favorite with local patrons, who consider this quaint restaurant and saloon the "in" place to dine.

Up Your Alley is located at 222 "The Alley" in downtown Aiken. The restaurant is open Monday through Saturday. Lunch is served from 11:30 a.m. until 2:30 p.m. Dinner is served from 5:30 p.m. until 10:00 p.m. Meals are served in the saloon from 11:30 a.m. until 2:00 a.m. For reservations (recommended for dinner) call (803) 649–2603.

UP YOUR ALLEY'S BEER BATTER PICKLES

12 ounces dark bottled beer
2½ cups all-purpose flour
½ teaspoon salt
pepper to taste

dash Worcestershire sauce
12 large kosher dill pickle
    spears
1 cup cooking oil

In a medium bowl, add beer and whip in 1½ cups of the flour with a whisk. Add salt, pepper and Worcestershire sauce and mix until batter is smooth. Set aside. Drain pickle spears and set aside. In a deep fryer, heat oil to 350 degrees. Dip pickles in the remaining flour, coating well, then dip them into beer batter. Place pickles in a frying basket and immerse in hot oil. Shake basket to prevent sticking, and cook pickles

119

until golden brown, approximately 3 to 5 minutes. Drain on paper towels and serve hot. The batter also may be used for frying fish or vegetables. Serves 4.

UP YOUR ALLEY'S VEAL PRINCESS

2 tablespoons clarified
   butter
8 ounces veal medallions
½ cup all-purpose flour
8 ounces bay scallops

¼ cup sherry
1 cup heavy cream
pinch tarragon
salt and pepper to taste

Melt butter in a 12-inch sauté pan. Dredge the medallions in flour and sauté in butter for 1 minute. Turn the veal over and add the scallops. Cook an additional 1 to 2 minutes. Remove veal and scallops from pan and set aside. Add sherry to the skillet to deglaze it. Add cream, tarragon, salt and pepper to pan. Reduce liquid until creamy, approximately 3 to 5 minutes. When ready to serve, divide veal and scallops into four portions, arranging scallops over medallions. Pour approximately ¼ cup of the cream sauce over each serving. Serves 4.

UP YOUR ALLEY'S THE ALLEY CAT

1½ ounces amaretto
2 ounces pineapple juice

3 ounces vanilla ice cream
6 ice cubes

Combine all ingredients in a blender container. Blend on high speed for 1 to 2 minutes. Serve in a brandy snifter. Serves 1.

THE WEST SIDE BOWERY
Aiken

**THE WEST SIDE
BOWERY**

It's hard to believe that the attractive area in downtown Aiken known today as "The Alley" was once a run-down haven for hoboes. The district has been handsomely restored and is now one of the city's most popular sightseeing spots.

One of the main attractions is The West Side Bowery. This restaurant and pub, the area's first renovation project, was the brainchild of Sam Erb. An energetic young man with a dream and lots of help from his family, Erb has managed to combine turn-of-the-century charm with an upbeat atmosphere.

The building, formerly a stable and carriage house, dates back to the late 1800s. Renovation was a long and difficult process, but worth the effort, as evidenced by the historic preservation award hanging near the entrance.

Creative ideas overflow in this inviting restaurant. On the day that I visited, the building's original exposed brick walls held the paintings of a local artist's first show. Three paintings had already been sold and it was barely noon. Another innovation is the "Erb Garden," which is a small private courtyard complete with umbrella-covered tables and a miniature garden.

My favorite dining area was the bright white and yellow porch. This is the ideal place to watch action in "The Alley." While sipping my iced tea, I could see sightseers browsing in shops and strolling in the miniature "Central Park." I had an excellent view of a mural of a Victorian home painted on the side of an adjacent building.

The aroma of good food prompted me to turn my attention from the sights to the menu. I was told that the Damon Steak Bits, Fried Okra and Zucchini are favorite appetizers. The Barrister, a sandwich of salami, Provolone and Cheddar cheese on an English muffin, is sure to please both lawyer and client.

For those who prefer seafood, let me suggest the Shrimp Salad plate. It was almost too pretty to tackle, but I dug in anyway. Their Vegetable Casserole, a blend of green beans, peas and limas in a creamy sauce, is superb.

There was more action in "The Alley" that warranted watching, but it was time for me to leave. I promised myself a return to The West Side Bowery during the evening hours when, I was told, a different but just as pleasing atmosphere awaits.

The West Side Bowery is located at 151 Bee Lane in downtown Aiken. Operating hours are from 11:30 a.m. until 1:00 a.m., Monday through Friday; and 11:30 a.m. until midnight on Saturday. For reservations (recommended for Friday night) call (803) 648–2900.

THE WEST SIDE BOWERY'S BARRISTER SANDWICH

1 English muffin	1 slice tomato
1 slice salami	1 slice Provolone cheese
1 slice Cheddar cheese	pinch of oregano

Split muffin in half. Add meat, Cheddar cheese and tomato. Top with Provolone cheese and sprinkle with oregano. Broil until cheese melts. Serves 1.

THE WEST SIDE BOWERY'S CHICKEN WINGS

1 cup sake	2 tablespoons brown sugar
¼ cup soy sauce	2 tablespoons water
1 clove garlic, crushed	3 to 5 pounds chicken wings

Combine sake, soy sauce, garlic, brown sugar and water in a saucepan. Heat and stir until well blended; do not boil. Pour sauce over chicken and marinate for 2 hours. Turn over once. Bake at 350 degrees until the chicken is brown and sauce is evaporated, about one hour. Serves 6 to 8 generously.

THE WEST SIDE BOWERY'S VEGETABLE CASSEROLE

1 10-ounce package frozen
peas
1 10-ounce package frozen
lima beans
1 10-ounce package frozen
green beans
1½ cups mayonnaise

1 medium onion, finely
chopped
1 teaspoon dry mustard
1 teaspoon Worcestershire
sauce
1 dash hot pepper sauce
3 hard-boiled eggs, chopped

Cook frozen vegetables in boiling water for 10 minutes; drain. Place vegetables in a casserole dish. In a medium bowl, combine remaining ingredients and mix well. Spread the sauce over the vegetables. Bake in a 350-degree oven until golden brown, about 20 to 30 minutes. Serves 4 to 6.

THE WEST SIDE BOWERY'S POUND CAKE

½ pound butter
½ cup shortening
3 cups sugar
5 eggs

3 cups all-purpose flour
1¼ cups milk
1 teaspoon vanilla

Cream butter, shortening and sugar together in a medium bowl. Add eggs, one at a time, beating well with an electric mixer. Alternately add the flour and milk, blending well. Add the vanilla and stir to combine. Pour into a greased and floured bundt pan or a 3-quart baking dish. Bake at 325 degrees for one hour and five minutes. Yields 1 cake.

THE VILLAGE INN RESTAURANT
Edgefield

THE VILLAGE INN RESTAURANT

Some old hotels never die. They live on, retaining a dignified status through all the change and turmoil that each new decade brings. The Plantation House, a stately red brick structure that dates back to the turn of the century, is just such a place.

Surprisingly, the hotel's restaurant, known as The Village Inn, originally was designed as a cafeteria where guests helped themselves. This informal manner of dining came to a halt in 1959 when Mrs. William Mims assumed ownership and operation of the historic hotel and restaurant. She had other ideas concerning the way dinner guests should be treated. Mrs. Mims believes that when you go out for a meal, you deserve pampering, and good old-fashioned pampering is just what you'll get when you dine in this gracious Southern environment.

You'll be intrigued with the restaurant's functional use of antiques. Many of the table bases are antique sewing machines and tea carts. A more formal dining area is located to the left of the main dining room. This room's sparkling crystal chandelier illuminates wall murals that depict antebellum riverboat scenes.

The menu at The Village Inn is as inviting as the atmosphere. Only lunch is served, and I think I can understand the reason for this. If you can finish all the homemade goodness on your plate, you won't be able even to think about dinner.

Sandwiches and salads are favorite luncheon items, and you'll be pleased at the reasonable prices. But in tribute to Mrs. Mims' husband, who enjoys a more substantial lunch when he strolls over from his newspaper office, there are selections called Special Additions. These dishes are for those who prefer heavier midday fare, such as London Broil with Whipped Potatoes, vegetables, bread and butter. And don't forget about soup, because this restaurant serves some of the best around.

For those interested in counting calories, the restaurant offers the Two Hundred 25. This cold plate of shrimp and sliced beef or chicken is surrounded by tomatoes, peaches, cottage cheese and melba toast. This is for the guest who wants to order a satisfying lunch that deletes calories, not taste!

As I watched fresh Apple Pie, Strawberry Cheesecake and an old-fashioned Banana Split pass my table, I was very tempted. But I focused my attention on the nostalgic tinkling melodies that came from an old player piano. I sat back, sipped my lemonade and thought of the Old South that has almost disappeared. A piece of it is preserved at The Village Inn.

The Village Inn Restaurant is located inside the Plantation House on Courthouse Square in downtown Edgefield. Lunch is served from 11:30 a.m. until 2:30 p.m., Monday through Friday. Reservations are unnecessary, but the telephone number is (803) 637–3313.

THE VILLAGE INN RESTAURANT'S LONDON BROIL WITH MUSHROOM GRAVY

½ cup vinegar
½ cup salad oil
½ teaspoon Worcestershire
  sauce
¼ teaspoon rosemary
¼ teaspoon basil
¼ teaspoon garlic salt
1½ to 2 pounds beef flank
  steak

3 tablespoons butter
¾ pound fresh mushrooms,
  sliced
3 tablespoons all-purpose
  flour
2 cups beef stock
½ teaspoon Kitchen
  Bouquet
salt and pepper to taste

Combine vinegar, oil, Worcestershire sauce, rosemary, basil and garlic salt in a glass or aluminum bowl. Marinate flank steak in this mixture overnight. Remove meat from marinade and slice it diagonally into thin slices. Grill, braise or broil the meat until done. Keep warm.

Melt butter in a sauté pan. Add sliced mushrooms and sauté until tender, about 3 to 5 minutes. Remove mushrooms and set aside. Blend flour into the butter until smooth. Stir in beef stock and cook until gravy is very hot and thick. Add the cooked mushrooms to the gravy. Color with the Kitchen Bouquet and salt and pepper to taste. Serve gravy over beef. Serves 4.

THE VILLAGE INN RESTAURANT'S
TURKEY NOGGIN

1 teaspoon commercial
  chutney
½ teaspoon peanut butter
2 slices whole wheat bread

3 slices turkey breast
1 slice Muenster cheese
2 slices pineapple

Blend chutney and peanut butter with a fork. Spread mixture on each slice of bread. Layer turkey, cheese and pineapple between the two slices. Broil until cheese is melted, about 2 to 3 minutes. Serves 1.

THE VILLAGE INN RESTAURANT'S
COUNTRY INN SPECIALTY

¼ pound ground chuck
1 hamburger bun
2 slices crisply fried bacon
2 lettuce leaves

1 slice tomato
1 slice American or Swiss
  cheese
2 teaspoons mushrooms

Shape ground chuck into a patty and broil until done. Slice bun in half and add beef patty. Top with bacon, lettuce, tomato, cheese and mushrooms. Serves 1.

THE NEWS AND HERALD TAVERN
Winnsboro

**THE NEWS AND
HERALD TAVERN**

The News and Herald Tavern is located in a handsome building considered to be a perfect example of nineteenth-century architecture. Listed in the National Register as Thespian Hall, this impressive red brick structure gets that name from the upstairs auditorium where pre-Civil War dramas, vaudeville acts, concerts and operas once were staged. The first level of the building served as a railway station during that period.

Eventually, the building became the headquarters of Fairfield County's weekly newspaper—*The News and Herald*. The editorial offices occupied the premises for 139 years. Today, it's the breakfast and lunch dishes that make the headlines here.

It was gray and dismal when I arrived at the restaurant, so I was grateful for the tavern's cozy, cheerful interior. Once I set foot on the black and white checkerboard floor and took a whiff of the good, homecooked victuals, my cloudy disposition disappeared. Old theater posters and antique props are scattered throughout the restaurant. A real showstopper is the stained-glass panel that hangs in the front window, but my applause goes to a carving of Epicurus, the Greek philosopher who was fond of good eating.

And speaking of good eating, I learned the meaning of Up Country cooking when I tasted the fruits of the culinary skills of partners Polly Parker and Betty Gutschlag. They advised me that sandwiches are their specialty, and you will find many listed on the printed menu. I chuckled at the name Tavern Misprint, a sandwich that includes just about everything in the deli case. The Chicken Salad had been highly recommended, and I agree, there is something special about this creamy combination of chicken chunks, eggs and mayonnaise. The reason for the salad's rave reviews is said to be the addition of chicken stock. You'll be able to try it for yourself, as Polly was eager to share her secret with us.

I was surprised to find so many items listed on the menu. You will find breakfast selections as well as pastries, ice cream treats and the beer and wine that give this restaurant the right to call itself a tavern.

The tavern is located in the historic district, so be sure to allow some browsing time before or after your meal. The Old Town Clock at the end of the street is said to be the oldest continuously running town clock in the United States.

The News and Herald Tavern is located at 114 East Washington Street in Winnsboro. Hours are from 8:30 a.m. until 3:30 p.m., Monday through Saturday. Reservations are unnecessary, but the telephone number is (803) 635-1331.

THE NEWS AND HERALD TAVERN'S
CHICKEN SALAD

1 3- to 4-pound chicken	½ cup chicken stock
2 hard-boiled eggs, chopped	½ cup mayonnaise
2 stalks celery, chopped	salt to taste
½ cup chopped sweet pickles	¼ teaspoon curry powder

Cover chicken with water in a soup pot and boil 1 to 1½ hours until very tender. Remove chicken from water and let cool. Reserve ½ cup of the chicken stock. Remove chicken from bones, and tear into small strips. Combine chicken with remaining ingredients and mix thoroughly with a wooden spoon. Serves 8 to 10.

THE NEWS AND HERALD TAVERN'S
LEMON CRUMB SQUARES

1 15-ounce can condensed milk	1 teaspoon baking powder
½ cup lemon juice	½ teaspoon salt
1 teaspoon grated lemon rind	⅔ cup butter
1½ cups sifted all-purpose flour	1 cup dark brown sugar
	1 cup uncooked oatmeal

In a small bowl, blend together milk, lemon juice and rind; set aside. In another bowl, sift together flour, baking powder and salt. In a large bowl, cream butter and blend in sugar. Add oatmeal and the flour mixture, and mix until crumbly. Spread half of the mixture in a 8- by 12- by 2-inch buttered baking pan and pat down. Spread condensed milk mixture over top; cover with remaining crumb mixture. Bake at 350 degrees for about 25 minutes, until brown around edges. Cool in the pan at room temperature for 15 minutes. Cut into 2-inch squares, and chill in the pan until firm. Yields 24 squares.

THE NEWS AND HERALD TAVERN'S
MISPRINT SANDWICH

1 8-inch hoagie roll	1 slice Swiss cheese
2 tablespoons mayonnaise	1 slice American cheese
2 slices ham	½ cup shredded lettuce
2 slices cotta salami	2 to 3 slices tomato
3 slices Genoa salami	3 thin slices onion
2 slices turkey	1 tablespoon commercial
2 strips bacon, cooked	Italian salad dressing
1 slice roast beef	

Split hoagie roll lengthwise. Spread mayonnaise on both sides. Alternately layer meats and cheeses. Top with lettuce, tomatoes and onions. Sprinkle salad dressing over all. Serves 1.

THE SIDE PORCH
Lancaster

THE SIDE PORCH **B**ack in the "dark ages" (when my children think I went to school) there was no thought of coed dormitories or of passing the dorm mother with alcohol on your breath. Those memories helped me identify with former boarders of Mrs. Walter Stevens, the grand dame dorm mother who kept male boarders in her home in Lancaster. The white frame house, built in 1925 by Mr. Stevens, is now a fine restaurant.

Mrs. Stevens' presence lingers in the tales told by former tenants who dine at The Side Porch today. Every boarder was obliged to adhere closely to the decorum of the household. Mrs. Stevens insisted upon a nonnegotiable curfew and would wait in her parlor rocking chair for the entrance of each young gentleman. If the young man had imbibed an alcoholic beverage, he had better give an Oscar-winning display of sobriety, as each who passed her chair was expected to be steady on his feet.

Feeling that my teetotaling grandmother was looking down upon me, I bypassed a glass of rosé and ordered a cup of hot spiced tea, which I sipped as I admired the décor. The downstairs dining room in which I sat featured forest-green tablecloths and elegant fan-shaped window dressings in matching shades of green. Adjacent to my table was a gigantic rosewood piano that serves as a salad bar, great for dieters since they can monitor their own caloric intake. Dieters also might choose the Bananadana Split, an attractive combination of bananas and other fresh fruits.

The Side Porch excels in the artistic presentation of food, whether served in the dining room or packaged for a take-out order. What can look more appealing in February than a Strawberry Spinach Salad? The only thing that beat the appearance was the taste. I also nibbled on their German Potato Salad and sampled Zucchini Muffins. When my quiche arrived, I decided to ask for the recipe but was told, "You don't want that; it's just a plain old Lorraine." True, I try to get the most unusual recipes, but this Quiche Lorraine was so exceptional that I hope it is the special when you visit.

I chose to take dessert upstairs and climbed past green silk moiré walls adorned with decorative objects for sale. As on the bottom floor, each upstairs room exudes an individual charm. My rich and delicious Derby Pie (which the proprietor gave to President Reagan when he was in Lancaster) was served in a room decorated with paintings by an artist who, like Grandma Moses, picked up the paint brush after her seventieth birthday.

One of my goals is to find recipes that are not only tasty, but unique as well. This restaurant made recipe selection very difficult, because everything I tasted was unique. The food, like the décor, is a class act.

The Side Porch is located at 308 West Dunlap Street in Lancaster. Lunch is served from 11:30 a.m. until 2:30 p.m., Monday through Friday. For reservations (preferred) call (803) 285-6660.

THE SIDE PORCH'S DERBY PIE

2 eggs, beaten
½ cup plus two tablespoons flour
½ teaspoon salt
1 cup sugar
1 stick butter (no substitute), melted and cooled

1 6-ounce package chocolate chips
¾ cup chopped pecans
1½ teaspoons vanilla
1 tablespoon bourbon
1 unbaked 9-inch pie shell
1 cup whipped cream

Beat eggs; combine them with the flour, salt and sugar in a bowl and mix well. Add butter, chocolate chips, pecans, vanilla and bourbon. Stir thoroughly until well blended. Pour into pie shell and bake in a 325-degree oven for 45 to 50 minutes. Serve warm with a dollop of whipped cream atop each serving. Yields 1 pie.

THE SIDE PORCH'S STRAWBERRY SPINACH SALAD
WITH POPPY SEED DRESSING

1¼ cups sugar
¼ cup honey
2 teaspoons dry mustard
2 teaspoons salt
3 tablespoons onion juice
⅔ cup wine vinegar

2 cups salad oil
3 teaspoons poppy seeds
1 pound fresh spinach
1 pint fresh strawberries,
   stemmed and sliced

In a blender container, add first six ingredients and blend for 5 to 10 seconds. Add oil gradually and continue blending until dressing is thickened. Add poppy seeds and chill. Wash, drain, and thoroughly dry spinach leaves. Tear into bite-sized pieces and top with strawberry slices. Before serving, add poppy seed dressing. Makes 8 servings.

THE SIDE PORCH'S GERMAN POTATO SALAD

4 large baked potatoes,
   chilled
4 strips bacon
¼ cup chopped bell pepper
½ cup chopped onion

1 tablespoon chopped
   parsley
1 cup sugar
¾ cup cider vinegar

Peel and slice potatoes. Set aside. In a skillet, fry bacon and remove, reserving grease. Add peppers, onions and parsley, and sauté in bacon grease until tender. Add sugar and vinegar; bring to a boil. Cook, stirring, until sugar is dissolved. Pour over potatoes, add bacon and toss until flavors are blended. Makes 4 to 6 servings.

THE CORNERSTONE INC.
Rock Hill

THE CORNERSTONE INC.

Do you believe in mental telepathy? Sue Waataja and Bliss Durkee, owners of The Cornerstone Inc., won't admit they believe in this method of communication, but they do. They met at a Newcomer's Gourmet Club meeting after both had moved to Rock Hill from the North. It was there that they discussed the area's lack of good restaurants. After a year of friendship and considerable market research, they decided to open a restaurant together.

It soon became apparent that communication was occurring between them without verbalization. At first it was laughed off as coincidence. But when they realized they were planning complete, often identical, meals without the exchange of one word, they knew it was more than "sympatico" thoughts.

The two-story building, built around 1919, used to function as a corner store. Bliss explained that the exposed brick inner walls were constructed from ballast found in the Charleston harbor. The rustic walls run up to the second floor dining area, which is well-lighted, with red geraniums in the spacious windows. My vote is cast for the adjoining dining room and its massive skylight. A profusion of ferns gives the illusion of a tropical setting.

The entire restaurant transmits a feeling of serenity that acts as a relaxing potion to the harried business people who schedule special trips to Rock Hill for The Cornerstone's Crab Bisque. After sampling a few bites, I understood their enthusiasm. Sue said the Bisque originally was offered once a week, but the restaurant was so mobbed on that day that the dish became a regular item.

People also come out of their way to eat the restaurant's Blueberry and Strawberry Gems. I tried both kinds of muffins and prefer the strawberry. Their concoction of Chicken Salad is so special that you'll find the recipe listed. Since so many dieters dine here, the owners offer a Garden Salad Pocket Sandwich with a choice of two low-calorie dressings, as well as a check list of salad ingredients that enables you to control your own caloric intake.

Of course, no one diets all the time. I proved this by speedily consuming their Fudge Walnut Pie a la Mode. Another quick and tasty dessert is the Banana Éclair, tucked inside a croissant. I included it with the recipes for times when you can't treat yourself to a visit to this restaurant.

The Cornerstone Inc. is located at 123 Elk Avenue in Rock Hill. Lunch is served from 11:00 a.m. until 3:00 p.m., Monday through Saturday. For reservations (preferred for parties of five or more) call (803) 328–3131.

THE CORNERSTONE INC.'S BANANA ÉCLAIR

Hot Fudge Sauce:

2 squares unsweetened baking chocolate
⅓ cup butter or margarine

4 tablespoons sugar
1 cup heavy cream
2 teaspoons vanilla extract

Melt chocolate and butter over low heat, stirring to blend. Add sugar and stir until completely dissolved. Add heavy cream, stirring to combine. Remove from heat. Add vanilla and stir until well mixed. Set aside.

Éclair:

4 commercial croissants
2 sliced bananas

1 3-ounce package vanilla pudding (follow package directions)

Split croissants and evenly divide sliced bananas among each pocket. Spoon in desired amount of vanilla pudding, and drizzle Hot Fudge Sauce over top. Serves 4.

THE CORNERSTONE INC.'S CHICKEN SALAD

⅓ cup heavy whipping cream
1 cup mayonnaise
6 cups cooked, diced chicken
1 cup diced celery

salt and pepper to taste
lettuce leaves
1 tomato, cut into wedges
olives
1 hard-boiled egg, sliced

Whip the cream and gently fold in mayonnaise. Add cooked chicken and celery; salt and pepper to taste. Chill thoroughly. Serve on lettuce leaves and garnish with tomato wedges, olives and slices of hard-boiled egg. Serves 8 to 10.

THE CORNERSTONE INC.'S STRAWBERRY GEMS

1 cup self-rising flour	**¼ cup milk**
¾ cup sugar	**¼ cup vegetable oil**
1 egg, beaten	**½ cup sliced strawberries**

Topping:
¼ cup sugar	**¼ teaspoon cinnamon**

Mix all ingredients except strawberries until thoroughly incorporated. Fold in strawberries, and fill paper-lined muffin tins ⅔ full. Combine sugar and cinnamon; sprinkle over top of muffins. Bake at 375 degrees for 20 to 25 minutes until lightly browned. Yields 18 muffins.

NOTE: Blueberries may be substituted for the strawberries.

THE HOMEPLACE
Rock Hill

THE HOMEPLACE Mr. Bates told me to crack my window before arriving at The Homeplace so my senses would be properly awakened to the "best barbecue in South Carolina." Even though it was raining, the elements couldn't compete with the rich aroma of the Bateses' pit-cooked barbecue. That fragrance is announced long before you see the massive magnolia that shelters the white frame farmhouse.

As I walked through the dining rooms of The Homeplace, it was difficult to believe this structure once was slated to burn in a practice session for the local fire department. Fortunately, the Bates family bought the property, which included the 150-year-old house. Mr. Bates and his son, Hugh, went about the arduous task of repairing the sixteen-inch, hand hewn timber walls and ceilings, which were still held intact with the original wood pegs. Of course, necessity called upon the Bateses to make several changes, so the heart pine floor you walk on today was once a wall.

Mrs. Bates has used simple muslin curtains at the tall windows, which are softened by large, hanging green plants. The fireplaces, each one original to the building, are adorned with interesting items. The former kitchen offers a banquet of goodies for diners to help themselves.

With little prodding, I helped myself to Barbecued Chicken, Ribs and Chopped Barbecue that had been "nursed" for fourteen hours over a pit. You may choose a tomato- or mustard-based sauce (I chose both) along with real homemade Cole Slaw and tangy Baked Beans. My absolute favorite was a dish called Hash. Although I begged for this recipe, which the Bateses call "feisty enough to make you slap your mother-in-law," it was the one secret with which they refused to part. Don't skip this "feisty" concoction when you visit.

The barbecue was so exceptional that I would have been laden with guilt had I not taken a few pounds home. The Bateses prepared a take-out order for my eager family, as they will for yours.

While my order was being prepared, I learned that the Bates family does not turn away hungry guests who are temporarily short of funds. "We believe in trust, and what we do here is to put that trust back into the American system," said Hugh. A record is made of the person's debt and is pinned out of sight near the cash register. When the customer returns he is on his honor to make good on the previous bill. Naturally, this practice prompted the question, "How often do you get stuck?" The proud answer was, "It has yet to happen."

The deed of sale restricts the sale of alcoholic beverages, but iced drinks fill in very nicely. When I return next summer, I'll sit outside under that magnificent magnolia and sip on lemonade while savoring those Ribs and Hash.

The Homeplace is located in Rock Hill on Highway 161 West. Meals are served from 11:00 a.m. until 9:30 p.m., Thursday, Friday and Saturday. Reservations are unnecessary, but the telephone number is (803) 366–2143.

THE HOMEPLACE'S RIBS WITH BARBECUE SAUCE

1 quart catsup	½ teaspoon salt
½ cup white vinegar	½ teaspoon pepper
½ cup dark brown sugar	3 to 4 pounds ribs
⅛ teaspoon paprika	

Pour catsup and vinegar into a large saucepan over medium heat. Add sugar and stir to remove any lumps. Add paprika, salt and pepper. Stir until flavors have combined and sauce has cooked, approximately 5 minutes. (Water may be added for a thinner sauce.)

Place ribs in a large, flat-bottomed glass bowl, and cover with sauce. Cover with foil and refrigerate for 8 to 24 hours. Remove ribs and grill or bake, basting with sauce frequently until done. Serves 4.

NOTE: The sauce also may be used for chicken.

THE HOMEPLACE'S BAKED BEANS

1 32-ounce can pork and
beans
½ cup brown sugar

¼ cup prepared mustard
¼ cup chopped onions
1 cup catsup

Combine all ingredients, mixing well. Place in an oven-proof, 1½- to 2-quart greased casserole. Bake in a 350-degree oven for 45 minutes. Serves 6 to 8.

THE HOMEPLACE'S COLE SLAW

2 small heads of cabbage
2 carrots

1 cup chopped sweet
pickles
1½ cups mayonnaise

Grate cabbage and carrots coarsely and place in a large bowl. Add pickles, and bind with mayonnaise. Cover and refrigerate until cool. Serves 10 to 12.

MOLLY MORGAN'S FINE EATING
ESTABLISHMENT
Chester

MOLLY MORGAN'S

An oasis atop the hill. That's how school children thought of Chester's Drugstore in 1902 and in years following. They knew that, once the climb was made, their cool reward would come from the drugstore's soda fountain.

A trudge up the same hill today yields a different reward. The seventeen-foot high, pressed-metal ceiling is still there. The difference is that crystal chandeliers and ceiling fans have added a touch of class to the eating establishment known as Molly Morgan's. Unfortunately, the original red, green, black and white tile floor is gone. Someone covered the tile with two inches of cement. The current proprietors would love to remove it, but professionals advise that most of the tile would be ruined in the process. Doing the next best thing, they have carpeted the floor in the original colors.

A collection of one-hundred-year-old portraits of the area's formerly prominent citizens decorates the walls of the restaurant. Some of the portraits are old tin-types embellished with pen, ink or pencil.

When I visited, the restaurant had only been open for two months, but it was already known for its Chili and Pizza. The Chili isn't the Texas-style chili I am accustomed to, but it is a hearty concoction worthy of the recipe section. My favorite dish is a hot sandwich called Molly's Tuna Casserole Sandwich. It combines tuna with mushrooms and black olives on a hoagie topped with melted Cheddar cheese and asparagus.

In the booth adjacent to me, I saw two women share the largest stuffed potato I'd ever seen. When they discovered my project, a sample was offered for testing. It was wonderful and could be considered a meal in itself.

If your bathing suit has quit on you, then you might think about ordering The Secretary Salad. It's a bounty of roast beef, ham, turkey, onions, peppers, mushrooms, olives, cheese and pepperoncini, served with a low-calorie dressing. If that doesn't suit your appetite, then try a Rib Eye and one of the homemade Cheesecakes, and jog down the hill afterward.

Many of the patrons were having a glass of beer or wine with their lunch, but since I was driving I concluded my samplings with coffee and a smidgen of Cheesecake.

Molly Morgan's is located at 132 Main Street in Chester. Lunch is served from 11:30 a.m. until 2:30 p.m., Monday through Saturday. Dinner is served from 5:00 p.m. until 9:00 p.m., Monday through Thursday, and until 11:00 p.m. on Friday and Saturday. For reservations (recommended for large parties) call (803) 377–3400.

MOLLY MORGAN'S TUNA CASSEROLE SANDWICH

1 6½-ounce can tuna fish
3 tablespoons mayonnaise
3 tablespoons sliced
  mushrooms
5 coarsely chopped black
  olives

2 hoagie rolls
commercial thousand island
  dressing
6 tablespoons grated
  Cheddar cheese
4 asparagus spears

Drain tuna well and put it in a small bowl. Add mayonnaise, mushrooms and black olives, mixing until well combined. Split hoagie rolls in half, and spread each with thousand island dressing. Distribute tuna mixture evenly over each roll. Divide cheese over each half and top with asparagus. Place hoagie rolls on a baking sheet and bake 4 to 5 minutes in a 500-degree oven until the hoagie browns. Serves 4.

MOLLY MORGAN'S STUFFED POTATOES

4 12- to 16-ounce baking
  potatoes
butter-flavored salt
8 teaspoons chopped onions
8 teaspoons chopped
  mushrooms
6 tablespoons grated
  Cheddar cheese

1 slice roast beef, chopped
1 slice ham, chopped
1 slice turkey, chopped
1 slice Kielbasa, chopped
6 tablespoons sour cream
2 teaspoons chives, fresh or
  frozen
4 cherry peppers

147

Bake potatoes in a 400-degree oven for 1 hour or until done. Split each potato in half, and carefully scoop out interior, leaving a ¼-inch shell. Break up potatoes with a fork and mound inside the potato skins. Sprinkle potatoes with butter-flavored salt, and add 2 teaspoons onions and 2 teaspoons mushrooms to each. Top each with 1½ tablespoons cheese, and place in a 500-degree oven for 4 to 6 minutes. Remove and top with chopped roast beef, ham, turkey and Kielbasa. Return to oven and cook 4 to 5 minutes. Remove and top each with 1½ tablespoons sour cream, ½ teaspoon of chives and a cherry pepper. Serves 4 generously.

MOLLY MORGAN'S CHILI

2 tablespoons corn oil
2 medium onions, chopped
4 garlic cloves, finely
  minced
1 pound ground chuck
dash of ground cloves
salt and pepper to taste
dash of red pepper flakes
¼ teaspoon ground cumin
1 bay leaf
1 tablespoon chili powder
½ teaspoon oregano

dash of celery salt
6 teaspoons tomato paste
1½ cups canned tomatoes
  with juice
1 pound cooked pinto beans
1 to 2 cups beef broth,
  coffee or beer (optional)
½ cup grated Cheddar
  cheese
⅓ cup sour cream for
  garnish

In a large, heavy Dutch oven, heat oil and sauté onions and garlic until wilted, about 3 minutes. Break up meat and add to mixture, stirring to break up lumps. Add cloves, salt, pepper, red pepper flakes, cumin, bay leaf, chili powder, oregano and celery salt. When mixture is well combined, add tomato paste and tomatoes with juice. Stir until thoroughly mixed; add beans. Lower heat and cook about 1 hour. If chili becomes too thick, add 1 to 2 cups of beef broth, coffee or beer. Serve with cheese sprinkled over top. Add a dollop of sour cream if desired. Serves 4 to 6.

GRAYSTONE STEAK HOUSE
Laurens

GRAYSTONE
STEAK HOUSE

When Graystone Steak House was recommended to me as a historic restaurant I should visit, the name immediately conjured up the image of a rustic, old home built of large, gray stones. So strong was this image that I passed right by the restaurant. Graystone didn't resemble my preconceived idea at all.

What I found was an impressive white mansion with stately pillars and a porch that wraps halfway around the building. This grand house was built in the early 1900s for the Gray family, after whom the restaurant is named, and it was their home until the early 1960s.

When Tom and Barbara Fischer purchased the mansion in 1968, it was all but hidden behind a thick cover of ivy. As the Fischers began the tedious process of transforming the former residence into a restaurant, it quickly became apparent that they had taken on more of a task than they had anticipated. Even though no major structural changes were required, the renovation process still took the family a year of full-time work to complete.

While the Fischers worked at restoring the mansion's lower level, their son Bob and his young friends enjoyed playing in the unoccupied rooms upstairs. One of their favorite rooms was the billiard room, which contained a pool table left behind by the former owners. The youngsters discovered that, along with the pool table, a ghost was left behind—reportedly the spirit of old Mr. Gray. The gentleman allegedly enjoyed the game so much that he returned on certain occasions, after which the boys would discover all the balls mysteriously placed in their proper pockets. This mischief stopped when the pool table was removed and the billiard room converted into an office.

Upstairs at the restaurant today, you can enjoy an aperitif or an after-dinner nightcap in the comfortable bar and lounge area. You probably won't see a ghost, but you will find a relaxed and dignified atmosphere which echoes that of the dining rooms below.

My table was located beside a bay window in one of the restaurant's most attractive dining rooms. The thick red carpet creates a feeling of warmth, while flickering table candles and hanging baskets of ivy add pleasing touches. The black and white attire worn by waiters and waitresses lends an air of formality.

Graystone Steak House, as its name implies, specializes in beef, and these featured entrées do deserve the spotlight. All steaks are aged for up to five weeks, and I dare say you won't find a more tender cut. The combination plates of beef and seafood also are tempting choices. For those preferring a lighter meal, look under the menu section, "On the Lighter Side." Several seafood selections will satisfy your taste buds and won't overtax your calorie count.

I ordered the Steak and Shrimp, a duo that met my high expectations. I can't remember ever having a juicier or more tender cut of meat. I could have cut the petite Filet Mignon with my fork. Equally tasty was the heap of lightly fried Shrimp and the Consommé Rice, a welcome change from the usual potato. A small loaf of freshly baked bread, served on a wooden board, highlighted our meal.

Graystone Steak House is located at 1100 South Harper Street on Highway 221 South in Laurens. Dinner is served from 5:30 p.m. until 10:00 p.m., Monday through Saturday. For reservations (recommended) call (803) 984–5521.

GRAYSTONE STEAK HOUSE'S COMFORTING PUNCH

1½ ounces Southern
    Comfort
¾ ounce vodka
4 ounces orange juice
2 ounces pineapple juice

½ to 1 teaspoon Grenadine
    for color
1 cup crushed ice or small
    ice cubes
lemon slice for garnish

Pour all ingredients except the lemon and ice into a blender container. Blend until frothy. Pour into a slender glass filled with ice. Garnish with a lemon slice. Serves 1.

GRAYSTONE STEAK HOUSE'S GRAY MAN

1½ ounces Kahlúa
1½ ounces Bailey's Irish
  Cream Liqueur
½ to ¾ ounce vodka

2 to 3 ounces half and half
½ cup crushed ice
3 ounces whipped cream for
  garnish

Pour all ingredients except whipped cream into a blender container. Blend on high speed until well mixed. Pour into 2 brandy snifters. Top each serving with a dollop of whipped cream. Serves 2.

GRAYSTONE STEAK HOUSE'S CONSOMMÉ RICE

1 10-ounce can onion soup
1 10-ounce can beef
  consommé
1 teaspoon butter or
  margarine

½ cup canned, sliced
  mushrooms with liquid
2 cups uncooked converted
  rice

Combine soups and butter in a saucepan. Bring to a boil, then set aside. In a casserole dish, mix together mushrooms and rice. Pour soup mixture over rice. Bake, covered, in a 350-degree oven for 1 hour. Serves 8.

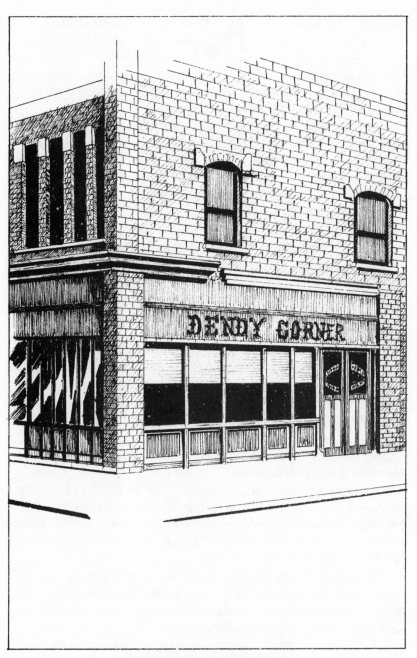

DENDY CORNER
Abbeville

DENDY CORNER No, Charles Dendy doesn't live here anymore. Over a century ago, Dendy decided the corner facing the town square was no longer a suitable site for his residence. So, he moved his home to a more desirable location, leaving behind only his name.

The next structure to rise on the corner vacated by Dendy was the Up Country's first liquor dispensary, built in 1884. Business flourished at the store until Prohibition came along to dampen spirits. A dispensary of another kind moved in during the 1930s when a filling station opened in the structure. Today the building houses Dendy Corner, a popular downtown attraction that contains all the ebullience of a neighborhood bar in a relaxed restaurant.

One of the restaurant's most interesting decorating features is the use of split levels. Management informed me that the raised lounge area conceals the former filling station's auto jack. I suppose this lends credence to the old adage, "Necessity is the mother of invention."

Other inventive ideas are used throughout this upbeat restaurant. Artfully chipped openings in the plaster walls permit a view of the original brick. Natural wood lattice-work partitions separate the bright dining room from the more intimate lounge, where the raised bar overlooks cozy booths. The blend of dark and light wood in the original oak ceiling, sturdy booths and butcher block tables complements the lustrous wood plank floors.

People-watchers would enjoy a table in the front dining room overlooking the action in The Square, with its charming brick-lined streets and Abbeville's historic opera house, now used for contemporary plays. The after-theater crowd often can be found dining at Dendy's.

The menu at Dendy Corner is as interesting as the atmosphere. Do-it-yourselfers can dictate the ingredients for their own sandwiches or stuffed potatoes. A variety of quiches, salads and cold plates are offered also.

I had heard about Dendy Corner's Potato Jackets and

decided to begin lunch with this appetizer. This is almost a meal in itself, so I shared with friends. They returned the favor and passed along the Nachos and spicy Jalapeño Cheese Dip. Olé to both.

For an entrée, I selected the Cheese Lover's Choice, a hefty slice of Cheddar and ham quiche, and found that it was too good to share. I managed to pass when dessert was offered, although the fresh, sweet concoctions—which vary from day to day—might overwhelm your willpower.

Dendy Corner is located on the corner of Pickens Street and South Main on The Square in downtown Abbeville. Meals are served from 11:30 a.m. until 9:45 p.m., Monday through Saturday. For reservations (recommended for dinner) call (803) 459–5800.

DENDY CORNER'S NACHOS

1 16-ounce package
  processed cheese
1 tablespoon mayonnaise
1 4-ounce can chopped
  green chilies

¼ cup minced chives
¼ cup finely diced tomatoes
Tabasco sauce to taste
½ pound tortilla chips

Cut cheese into small cubes and melt in top of double boiler. Add mayonnaise, chilies, chives and tomatoes and stir until thoroughly blended. Add Tabasco to taste. Serve warm with tortilla chips for dipping. Yields 2 cups.

DENDY CORNER'S GREAT POTATO HEAD

1 large baking potato
1½ tablespoons butter
1 ounce chopped ham
1 ounce chopped bacon

2 ounces grated Cheddar
  cheese
½ cup sour cream

Rub potato with 1 teaspoon butter and bake in a 375-degree oven for 1 hour. Slice potato lengthwise and add remaining butter, ham, bacon and cheese. Return to oven and bake at

400 degrees until cheese is melted. Top with sour cream before serving. Serves 1.

DENDY CORNER'S "H.T.B."

3 tablespoons mayonnaise
4 tablespoons German
  mustard
1 ounce white vinegar
¼ tablespoon curry powder
1 tablespoon onion salt

¼ tablespoon garlic powder
2 slices pumpernickel bread
1 ounce ham, thinly sliced
1 ounce turkey, thinly sliced
1 ounce bacon bits
2 slices Swiss cheese

Combine mayonnaise, mustard, vinegar, curry powder, onion salt and garlic powder in a small bowl. Mix well to blend flavors. Spread mixture on both slices of pumpernickel. Between bread, layer ham, turkey, bacon bits and cheese. Serves 1.

HARTZOG'S TEA ROOM
Gaffney

HARTZOG'S TEA ROOM

When it comes to gazebos, I admit to being a real push-over. You can imagine, then, my delight at finding a charming setting at Hartzog's Tea Room that is so sunny and intimate that I felt like I was lunching in a real gazebo. You can't help but feel like Alice in Wonderland after stepping into the Garden Room, where wisteria and Spanish moss hang from a trellised ceiling that sparkles with miniature lights. Palm-printed walls peek from behind white lattice panels. Wicker chairs and tables are covered in pastel print tablecloths.

The Gourmet Room, with its country setting, is every bit as inviting as the Garden Room. Williamsburg wall coverings and Windsor chairs decorate the room, and an interesting collection of gourmet kitchen and pantry items fills the handsome baker's racks and one whole wall of shelves.

The tea room's tempting luncheon menu ranges from salads to Stuffed Spuds and New York Strip Steaks. I was pleased to find several selections with the calorie count listed, a welcome aid for dieters. The house favorite, a creamy Chicken Salad served with sliced fruit, became my favorite too. When the basket of Applesauce Muffins arrived, it was easy to understand why customers threw a fuss when the proprietors tried to introduce a different bread. They were the best I've eaten anywhere. You will be able to order them when you visit; the muffins are now a permanent part of Hartzog's fare. If you visit on the first weekend of any month, you can dine on live Maine lobsters, flown in specially for seafood enthusiasts.

I meandered through the Hartzog's general store on my way out. While there I discovered that the attractive two-story building which houses the tea room and store has been a familiar structure in Gaffney for over one hundred years. Originally built as an opera house, it later became a popular movie theater, attracting film devotees from miles around. Today, of course, Hartzog's attracts food buffs rather than film buffs, but they are just as enthusiastic as the moviegoers once were.

Hartzog's Tea Room is located at 400 North Limestone Street in Gaffney. Lunch is served from 11:00 a.m. until 2:00 p.m., Monday through Saturday. Reservations are not accepted, but the number is (803) 489–2244.

HARTZOG'S TEA ROOM'S DRIED BEEF SPREAD

8 ounces cream cheese, softened
1 2½-ounce jar dried beef, cut into small strips
2 scallions, finely chopped

1 tablespoon Worcestershire sauce
½ teaspoon monosodium glutamate or salt
assorted crackers

Combine all ingredients except crackers and mix thoroughly. Shape into a ball. Cover and chill for at least 2 hours. Remove from refrigerator a few minutes before serving to soften. Serve with crackers. Yields more than 1 cup.

HARTZOG'S TEA ROOM'S APPLESAUCE MUFFINS

1 stick margarine, melted
1 cup sugar
2 cups flour
1 cup applesauce
1½ teaspoons cinnamon

1 teaspoon allspice
½ teaspoon cloves
1 teaspoon baking soda
½ teaspoon vanilla
1 egg

Mix all ingredients together with an electric mixer. Fill paper-lined muffin tins ⅔ full. Bake at 350 degrees for 15 to 20 minutes until browned. Yields 18 muffins.

NOTE: This recipe may be doubled as the batter will keep, covered, in the refrigerator for 2 to 3 weeks.

HARTZOG'S TEA ROOM'S PEANUT BUTTER PIE

3 ounces cream cheese
¾ cup confectioners' sugar
⅓ cup milk
3 heaping tablespoons crunchy peanut butter

6 ounces nondairy whipped topping
1 9-inch graham cracker crust
commercial fudge sauce

Cream together cream cheese and confectioners' sugar with an electric mixer until blended. Add milk and peanut butter; mix thoroughly. Fold in whipped topping. Pour into graham cracker crust and freeze until firm. When ready to serve, heat fudge sauce and drizzle over each slice. Yields 1 pie.

HARTZOG'S TEA ROOM'S STEAK SAUCE

3 tablespoons butter
½ cup chopped fresh
  mushrooms
2 chopped scallions
½ tablespoon plain flour
pinch of marjoram
⅛ teaspoon pepper

1 minced garlic clove
1 10-ounce can beef broth or
  beef stock
1 tablespoon white wine
¼ cup red wine
1 tablespoon brandy
½ teaspoon salt

Melt 2 tablespoons of the butter in a skillet, and sauté mushrooms and scallions until clear. Make a paste of the remaining butter and flour in the top of a double boiler. Add marjoram, pepper and garlic. Slowly add beef broth and mix well. Add mushrooms and scallion mixture, stirring to incorporate. Simmer for 45 to 60 minutes. Stir in white wine, red wine, brandy and salt, and mix until heated through. Serve over steaks or hamburgers. Yields more than 1 cup.

THE PACE HOUSE
Spartanburg

THE PACE HOUSE   The Pace House goes "under-
cover" in the spring. Dur-
ing this season, huge weeping
cherry trees, camellias and flowering tulip trees nearly conceal
this lovely Victorian home from view.

When Debbie and Jerry Beasley purchased the abandoned
structure in the late 1970s, it was hard to see the old home's
beauty under the blanket of brambles and brush that spelled
many years of neglect. But this determined couple, armed
with an appreciation for historic preservation and a strong
desire to operate a restaurant, recognized this diamond in
the rough. After many months of polishing, the gem is shining
once again.

The home was built in 1890 for Matthew Heldeman, a
German harness maker. I have no doubt that Heldeman, who
moved from the home in the 1940s, would be proud to see
how carefully the current proprietors have restored the house.
Original woodwork and ornate fireplaces are combined with
interesting accessories throughout the restaurant. An authentic
English bakery sign hangs above the bar in the lounge. This
touch of yesteryear lends an informal feel to the more
traditional settings found in the dining rooms.

The Pace House offers traditional dishes on both the
luncheon and dinner menus. Such favorite entrées as Chicken
Kiev and Roast Prime Rib of Beef may be ordered to suit the
size of any appetite.

Since my dinner appetite was anything but petite, I ordered
Table d'Hote. A steaming cup of French Onion Soup was my
first course. The dark broth, swimming with onions and
topped with a slice of Provolone cheese, was as good as you'll
find anywhere. A crisp house salad followed, topped with a
nice variation of creamy ranch dressing and nuts. The Pièce
de résistance was the highly recommended Chicken Kiev, a
boneless breast of chicken oozing with garlic butter and
covered with a light cream sauce. Now I know why local
patrons insist that this entrée appear on both the lunch and
dinner menus. Instead of potatoes, I selected Butter Cinnamon

Apples and Cream, which turned out to be so good I requested the recipe.

I chose a chilled chardonnay for my wine selection and applauded myself, not only for my choice, but because I even was able to make a decision. The wine list is a complete one and includes many favored domestic and imported wines. The same treatment is shown to beer lovers, as The Pace House offers an impressive selection of domestic and imported beers.

Dessert was not supposed to be in my plan, since I had finished each course with relish. But I changed my mind when I saw a creamy slice of Cheesecake. This old favorite contains a slight, refreshing hint of lemon, which made the concoction a perfect ending to a "well-Paced" meal.

The Pace House is located at 330 South Pine Street in Spartanburg. Lunch is served from 11:30 a.m. until 2:00 p.m., Monday through Friday. Dinner is served from 5:30 p.m., Monday through Saturday. Sunday buffet is served from 11:30 a.m. until 2:00 p.m. For reservations (recommended) call (803) 573–7669.

THE PACE HOUSE'S
BUTTER CINNAMON APPLES AND CREAM

½ stick butter or margarine
¾ cup sugar
¾ teaspoon cinnamon
¼ teaspoon nutmeg
1 tablespoon water

1 20-ounce can apple slices, water packed
1 cup whipped cream
4 maraschino cherries

Melt butter over low heat in a large saucepan. Add sugar and stir until dissolved. Mix in the spices and stir until well blended. Add the water, bringing the mixture to a slow simmer. Pour in the apples and packing juice; simmer and stir until heated through. Pour into individual serving bowls. Add a dollop of whipped cream to each serving, and top with a maraschino cherry. Serves 4.

THE PACE HOUSE'S CHICKEN KIEV

2 large boneless chicken
   breasts
2 tablespoons garlic butter,
   chilled
2 eggs
2 tablespoons milk

1 cup sifted all-purpose
   flour
salt and pepper to taste
½ cup bread crumbs
1½ to 2 cups oil for deep
   frying

Cream Sauce:
2 tablespoons butter
2 tablespoons flour

½ cup half and half
½ cup chicken broth

Flatten chicken breasts with a wooden mallet. Roll each breast around 1 tablespoon of garlic butter and secure with toothpicks. In a small bowl, combine the eggs with the milk and whip with a whisk until well blended. Season flour with salt and pepper in a separate bowl. Place bread crumbs in another bowl. Dip chicken first in egg mixture, then in flour. Dip again in egg mixture and roll in bread crumbs. Deep fry at 350 degrees until dark brown. To prepare sauce, melt butter in a sauté pan. Add 2 tablespoons flour, and stir constantly until smooth. Gradually add half and half and chicken broth; stir over low heat until sauce is thick. Before serving, remove toothpicks from chicken breast, and cover with sauce. Serves 2.

THE PACE HOUSE'S SPARTAN BURGER

6 ounces ground beef
2 tablespoons butter
½ cup chopped onions
½ cup sliced fresh
   mushrooms

½ cup grated sharp
   Cheddar cheese
¼ cup chopped scallions

Shape ground beef into a patty, and broil until done. Melt butter in a pan and sauté onions and mushrooms until tender. Pour vegetables over beef and top with cheese and scallions. Serves 1.

THE PIAZZA TEA ROOM
Spartanburg

THE PIAZZA
TEA ROOM

There is an enchanted place where summer lasts all year. It is a sparkling white porch, where ferns burst through hanging baskets and sunlight streams through high, arched windows. Although I was told that this serene back porch is irresistible during the spring when the dogwoods are in bloom, it couldn't have been more pleasing on the winter day of my visit.

I have often hoped to find a special place where I could take my Yankee friends when I want to show them what Southern grace and hospitality are all about. There is no need to look any longer, because as soon as I stepped into The Piazza Tea Room, I knew the search was over.

The historic structure that houses the tea room dates back to 1909. It has played many roles in Spartanburg's history. Local residents remember when the grand, old home was once a dormitory for students attending Converse College, located across the street. But the most prominent memory relates to the many times the home was used as a Halloween haunted house. Needless to say, ghosts and goblins would not be able to recognize the renovated building today.

Hues of bright peach set off the dazzling white ceiling, floor, tables and chair backs. This orange sherbet color is found in the floor stencils, the cloth place mats, the chair seats and in the napkins that are artistically tucked into water goblets.

The décor is not the only attraction in the tea room. The food is just as special. Each dish on the menu is explained in mouth-watering detail, so don't be surprised if you want to order everything listed. The Salmagundi, an eighteenth-century name for a chef salad, is a meal in itself. You'll also find soups, sandwiches, hot entrées and combination plates.

Because I was in the mood for sampling a variety of goodies, I ordered the Tea Sandwich Platter, a house specialty. It's obvious why this selection is so popular—it's a culinary work of art. I didn't want to make a dent in the Frozen Date Soufflé Salad, which was surrounded by petite tea sandwiches and fresh fruit, but after the first bite I forgot about art and attended to appetite.

Instead of wine or coffee, I chose a pot of spiced tea to complement my meal. If you have never had the pleasure of enjoying tea prepared this way, do yourself a favor and make it. This full-bodied brew was so good I asked for the recipe.

The tea room's grand finale is their incredible selection of homemade desserts. You won't find run-of-the-mill desserts here. There are pies with unusual names—Mud, Fox Head and Brownie, for instance—and cheesecakes flavored with chocolate chips, pralines or amaretto. I chose the Sawdust Pie, filled with pecans and coconut and topped with whipped cream, banana slices and a maraschino cherry.

The Piazza Tea Room is located on the corner of East Main Street and Mills Avenue in Spartanburg. Lunch is served from 11:30 a.m. until 2:00 p.m., Monday through Saturday. Beverages and desserts are served from 11:30 a.m. until 5:00 p.m., Monday through Saturday. For reservations (preferred) call (803) 585–0606.

THE PIAZZA TEA ROOM'S SAWDUST PIE

1½ cups sugar
1½ cups flaked coconut
1½ cups chopped pecans
1½ cups graham cracker
  crumbs
7 egg whites

1 unbaked 9-inch pie shell
1 cup whipped cream
1 sliced banana
maraschino cherries for
  garnish

Preheat oven to 350 degrees. Combine sugar, coconut, pecans and graham cracker crumbs in a medium bowl. Add unbeaten egg whites, and blend with a spoon until thoroughly mixed, but do not beat. Pour into the pie shell. Bake until filling is set, about 30 to 35 minutes. Serve warm or at room temperature. Top each serving with a dollop of whipped cream, a few banana slices and a stemmed cherry. Yields 1 pie.

THE PIAZZA TEA ROOM'S HOT SPICED TEA

4 quarts boiling water
5 family-size tea bags
1 12-ounce can frozen
   lemonade
1 6-ounce can frozen orange
   juice

1 12-ounce can pineapple
   juice
1¼ cups sugar
2 teaspoons whole allspice
lemon slices for garnish
1 teaspoon whole cloves

Add boiling water to tea bags; cover and steep for 10 minutes. Pour tea into a 30-cup electric percolator. Add thawed juices and sugar. Place spices in the basket of the percolator and perk until done. Serve hot, and garnish each serving with a lemon slice studded with whole cloves. Yields 1¼ gallons.

NOTE: For Spiced Iced Tea, fill a glass with ice. Pour tea into the glass until ⅔ full. Fill the remainder of the glass with cold ginger ale.

THE PIAZZA TEA ROOM'S
FROZEN DATE SOUFFLÉ SALAD

1 8-ounce package cream
   cheese
¼ cup maple syrup
2 medium-sized ripe
   bananas
1 tablespoon lemon juice

1 8-ounce can crushed
   pineapple, drained
½ cup finely chopped dates
½ cup finely chopped
   pecans
1 cup whipping cream

Allow cream cheese to soften and place it in a medium bowl. Beat syrup into cheese with an electric mixer. Mash the bananas and combine them with lemon juice; add to cream cheese and beat until thoroughly blended. Stir in pineapple, dates and pecans. Whip the cream and fold it into the soufflé mixture, and gently stir until well blended. Spoon into paper-lined muffin tins and freeze until firm. Allow to soften slightly before serving. Serves 12.

THE INN AT WASHINGTON
Greenville

THE INN AT WASHINGTON

How does a dream become a reality? I suppose the answer varies according to the situation, but it usually isn't a magical or effortless process. A lot of hard work goes into making a dream into a reality. This was certainly the case with The Inn at Washington. The idea for the inn was formed when Byran Carroll decided to try to recreate, in an old Southern setting, the warm feeling he enjoyed at his favorite New England vacation retreat. His intention was to create an elegant, relaxed atmosphere and combine it with fine cuisine and, after months of toil, he succeeded.

The stately, white structure, which today houses the restaurant on the first level and offers lodging upstairs, was built in 1911 on a site thirty-five feet away from its present location. When the house was moved in the 1920s, an enormous cellar was dug next door, and the house was transported by logs and set above it. Someday, Carroll hopes to transform the basement into an English-style country pub.

I arrived at the inn on a crisp autumn evening and was welcomed by the comforting smell of oak logs burning. Waiting was a pleasure in the handsome room that is referred to as the "library," where a gleaming baby grand piano often provides visitors with classical dinner music.

The restaurant's atmosphere speaks of well-mannered grace. Two of the five dining rooms are flushed with a color called "peach brandy." I was informed that this lovely rose tone enhances a woman's complexion. Can you guess where I asked to be seated?

The inn's menu offers continental cuisine and includes such appetizer favorites as Shrimp Scampi and Seviche. Entrées include Veal Maison, Oyster Fillet and Apricot Roast Duck. Feeling relaxed in such a leisurely and elegant atmosphere, I dismissed my caloric reticence and ordered the Poulet Sauté aux Champignons. This scrumptious chicken breast, stuffed with ham, mushrooms and cheese, arrived swimming in a creamy wine sauce. I also enjoyed the unbelievably tasty dinner rolls, which owe their doughnut-like flavor to the chef's deep fryer. The house white wine proved to be an excellent accompaniment to my meal, but the inn also provides a complete line of cocktails, liqueurs and imported and domestic wines.

Because I dined with such gusto, I had no room left for the "I Did It" Ice Cream Pie, a house specialty. Perhaps you *can* do it and finish the generously apportioned dessert. I comforted myself by bringing back the recipe and making it for my two sons, who practically inhaled the pie in one sitting.

The Inn at Washington is located at 1007 East Washington Street in Greenville. Lunch is served Tuesday through Friday from 11:45 a.m. until 2:00 p.m. Dinner is served from 6:00 p.m. until 10:00 p.m., Monday through Saturday. For reservations (recommended) call (803) 271–6672.

THE INN AT WASHINGTON'S
POULET SAUTE AUX CHAMPIGNONS

2 eggs	3 double chicken breasts (or
2 tablespoons milk	6 deboned)
½ cup plain flour	6 thin ham slices
2 tablespoons sesame seeds	1 cup sliced mushrooms
½ teaspoon salt	1 cup grated Swiss cheese
¼ teaspoon garlic salt	½ cup chicken broth
¼ teaspoon paprika	1 cup sour cream
2 tablespoons butter	½ cup dry white wine
1 tablespoon olive oil	

Combine eggs and milk in a bowl, mixing well. In another bowl combine flour, sesame seeds, salt, garlic salt and paprika, mixing until thoroughly blended. In a skillet, slowly melt butter and add olive oil. Bone, skin and split chicken breasts into 6 halves. Top each chicken breast with a slice of ham, a few slices of mushrooms and 1 tablespoon of cheese. Roll up each chicken breast, securing with toothpicks. Dip chicken rolls in egg mixture; follow by dipping in flour mixture. Brown chicken rolls evenly in butter and oil. Remove from pan and place in baking dish. Pour broth over chicken rolls and bake at 350 degrees for 30 minutes. Remove chicken rolls from casserole. Add remaining mushrooms to chicken drippings and simmer for 3 to 5 minutes. Blend in sour cream, wine and remaining cheese. Stir until thick and well blended. Place chicken rolls on serving platter and spoon sauce over top. Serves 5 to 6.

THE INN AT WASHINGTON'S "I DID IT" ICE CREAM PIE

1 8½-ounce box chocolate
   wafers
1 tablespoon sugar
¼ teaspoon cinnamon
¼ cup melted butter
1 quart vanilla ice cream
1 pint chocolate fudge ice
   cream

1 pint peppermint ice cream
¼ cup toasted almond slices
2 cups whipped cream
12 maraschino cherries
½ cup honey
¼ cup amaretto

Finely crush wafers in a food processor or blender. Add sugar, cinnamon and butter, and blend until well mixed. Press wafer mixture into sides and bottom of a buttered 9- or 10-inch springform pan. Bake crust in 350-degree oven for 8 to 10 minutes or until done. Set aside to cool. Press back any of the shell which may have pulled away while baking. Spread the three ice creams into the shell in layers, filling completely. Press toasted almonds on top of ice cream. Freeze for at least 6 hours. Remove from pan while firm and cut into 12 pieces. Place a large dollop of whipped cream on a plate, and stand pie slice up in center of whipped cream. Place another large dab of whipped cream over each slice and top with a cherry. Drizzle with honey and amaretto. Yields 1 pie.

SEVEN OAKS
Greenville

SEVEN OAKS

It was love at first sight when Martha and Al Rasche found this stately 1895 mansion. It didn't matter that the structure was all but hidden behind wisteria vines and brambles. After several months of extensive cleanup and renovation, the grand manor, named after the seven towering oak trees that surround it, opened its doors to the public.

Upon entering, I understood why Seven Oaks is considered Greenville's premier restaurant. It is evident that no expense was spared in the restoration. From the tastefully decorated dining rooms to the polished woodwork and restored rock maple floors, this restaurant is posh, with a capital "P."

Shades of brown, rose, burgundy and peach harmonize well in the six dining rooms and two lounges, yet each room has a distinctive décor. The chocolate-colored dining room in which I was seated had an air of contemporary drama.

Let me assure you that the dramatic interior isn't the only impressive feature at Seven Oaks. Making a dining decision from a menu listing such irresistible items as Mussels Mariniere, Chateaubriand Bouquetiere and Crustaces en Brochette proved to be an impossible undertaking. I chose to leave it to the chef and asked for his recommendation.

The presentation of the mouth-watering rack of lamb was as fine as the taste, which was enhanced by the addition of fresh mint to the sauce. My dining companion was trying to keep things light, so he ordered the Swordfish Almondine, sans the almonds. I couldn't have cared less about the calories when the dessert cart arrived. I sampled two tasty desserts. The Flourless Chocolate Cake was reminiscent of a light and luscious soufflé, while the Lemon Meringue Pie was one of the best I've ever tasted.

We were reluctant to leave such relaxing elegance. From the soft classical music to the flaming Crepes Suzette being served at a nearby table, our meal at Seven Oaks was a wonderful way to stimulate the senses—and that is what this restaurant does best.

Seven Oaks is located at 104 Broadus Avenue in Greenville. Dinner is served from 6:00 p.m. until 10:30 p.m., Monday through Saturday. For reservations (recommended) call (803) 232–1895.

SEVEN OAKS' FLOURLESS CHOCOLATE CAKE

9 ounces semisweet
chocolate
1 stick plus 1 tablespoon
butter
1 cup sugar

7 eggs, separated
2 tablespoons Grand
Marnier
confectioners' sugar for
dusting

Melt chocolate with butter in a double boiler. Add all but 2 tablespoons of the sugar, stirring until sugar is dissolved. In a separate bowl, beat egg yolks with a whisk until well blended, and stir 2 tablespoons of chocolate mixture into the yolks. Combine the yolk mixture with chocolate and butter in the double boiler. Add Grand Marnier and stir constantly until mixture becomes thick; remove from heat. Beat egg whites with an electric mixer until stiff. While beating, add remaining 2 tablespoons of sugar. Fold egg whites gently into chocolate mixture. Pour into buttered and floured 9½-inch springform pan. Bake at 250 degrees for 1½ hours. When cool, remove cake from pan and chill. (The top will fall and crack.) Dust with confectioners' sugar before serving. Yields 1 cake.

SEVEN OAKS' LAMB CHOPS WITH MINT SAUCE

½ teaspoon finely chopped
fresh spearmint
½ teaspoon finely chopped
fresh peppermint
¼ cup red wine vinegar

1 cup apple mint jelly
2 tablespoons butter
6 lamb chops
salt and pepper to taste

Combine the mints with vinegar in a small saucepan, stirring until blended. Cook over medium heat until reduced by half. Add jelly and boil the mixture for 10 minutes. Set aside.

Melt butter in a skillet and fry lamb chops until done. Salt and pepper to taste. Spread sauce over lamb chops before serving. Serves 6.

SEVEN OAKS' LEMON MERINGUE PIE

1½ cups milk
5 eggs, separated
¾ cup sugar
3½ tablespoons cornstarch
1 teaspoon unflavored
   gelatin

1 tablespoon cold water
juice from 2 lemons
grated rind from ½ lemon
1¼ cups confectioners'
   sugar
1 9-inch pie shell, baked

Bring milk to a boil in a saucepan. Set aside to cool. Beat egg yolks and ¼ cup of the sugar until mixture forms a ribbon. Add cornstarch and stir to blend. Add egg mixture to scalded milk; cook over low heat, stirring constantly until thickened. Dissolve gelatin in cold water and stir into hot milk mixture. Add lemon juice and grated rind to the mixture, blending with a spoon until well combined. Set aside to cool. With an electric mixer, beat egg whites until stiff. Add 2 tablespoons of granulated sugar during the beating process. Sift confectioners' sugar and remaining sugar together, and fold into beaten egg whites. Fold half of meringue into the lemon cream mixture. Pour into baked pie shell and chill until set. Before serving, top the chilled pie with remaining meringue and brown under the broiler. Yields 1 pie.

1109 SOUTH MAIN
Anderson

1109 SOUTH MAIN

One hardly expects to find the atmosphere of a South Pacific island in Anderson, South Carolina, but that is what waits behind the imposing white columns at 1109 South Main. Don't let the mansion's Greek Revival exterior fool you, because you're in for a delightful "tropical" experience. It begins as soon as you enter the gracious home, built in 1860 as a wedding present for the daughter of a prominent Anderson family.

The present owners, Peter and Myrna Ryter, spent four years in Tahiti before buying the mansion. They have managed to instill the laid-back mood of island life in this elegant two-story structure. Lush potted plants decorate the spacious entry hall. Soft music reminds you that this is not a place for those in a hurry. After all, does anyone hurry in the tropics?

The most interesting dining area is the Gauguin Room, named after the famous French artist who lived and worked in Tahiti. Many reproductions of the artist's work are displayed on the walls. Other treasures garnered during the owners' years in Tahiti include a colorful handmade Tahitian bedspread and a wall hanging constructed of coconut husks. Any beachcomber will admire the vast collection of seashells.

Impressed as I was with all the tropical furnishings, it should be no surprise to learn of my dinner choices. For my salad course, I chose the Hearts of Palm Bora Bora. It was everything I had hoped it would be—delicious and refreshingly different. Next came the Poisson Cru, an exotic treat of fresh fish chunks marinated in lime juice and coconut milk and served in a coconut shell. I couldn't say no to the Vegetable Mousse, a tasty slice of pureed cauliflower, broccoli and carrots molded into colorful layers, then wrapped in seaweed.

For those not as smitten with island fare, the menu also includes an ample selection of continental and American offerings. For lunch, you will find it hard to choose from the various soups, salads, sandwiches and tempting specialties such as Crepes, Wienerschnitzel and Tenderloin of Beef. Dinner selections are just as appealing. Such delicacies as Escargots and Avocado Ambrosia are featured appetizers.

Entrées include several choices of seafood and meats, and the wine list contains over fifty varieties of imported and domestic wines. For dessert, a daily selection of Tortes, Mousses, Caramel Creams and Fresh Berries is available.

1109 South Main is located at 1109 South Main in Anderson. Lunch is served from 11:30 a.m. until 2:00 p.m., Tuesday through Friday. Dinner is served from 6:00 p.m., Tuesday through Saturday. For reservations call (803) 225–1109.

1109 SOUTH MAIN'S POISSON CRU

2 pounds fresh tuna, swordfish, wahoo or grouper, deboned
8 limes
2 chopped tomatoes
1 grated carrot
1 chopped onion
1 finely chopped garlic clove
dash salt and pepper
dash hot pepper sauce
1 pint coconut milk
lettuce leaves for garnish

Cut fish into 1-inch by ½-inch pieces. Place fish pieces in a stainless or glass bowl and squeeze lime juice over them. Allow fish to marinate in juice for 10 minutes. Pour off the juice, draining well. Add vegetables, salt, pepper, hot pepper sauce and coconut milk. Mix well with a spoon, and serve on lettuce. Serves 4.

NOTE: Slices of hard-boiled egg and cucumber may be added, if desired.

1109 SOUTH MAIN'S ONION SOUP

4 onions
2 tablespoons cooking oil
1 bay leaf
dash monosodium glutamate
dash white pepper
½ teaspoon Worcestershire sauce
1 cup white wine
1 quart chicken broth or bouillon
4 to 6 slices bread
1 cup grated Swiss cheese

Peel onions; cut each in half and finely slice. In a soup pan, heat oil. Add onions and sauté until tender. Add bay leaf, monosodium glutamate, pepper and Worcestershire sauce; cook ingredients until onions are golden brown. Add wine and chicken broth and cook over medium heat for 10 minutes. Pour soup into individual oven-proof serving bowls and top each with a bread slice and 2 tablespoons of grated cheese. Place bowls under broiler until cheese is melted. Serves 4 to 6.

NOTE: The soup may be kept for days in the refrigerator and reheated before serving.

1109 SOUTH MAIN'S SALMON STEAK

2 tablespoons salted butter
4 4-ounce salmon steaks
12 medium shrimp, peeled
1 5-ounce can chopped
    clams
4 crawfish
dash white pepper

dash monosodium
    glutamate
1 cup white wine
2 teaspoons chopped
    parsley
½ cup heavy cream

Preheat oven to 350 degrees. In an oven-proof skillet, melt butter over medium heat. Add salmon and sauté slightly on one side, about 5 minutes. Turn salmon over and add shrimp, clams and crawfish to pan. Season with pepper and monosodium glutamate. Add the wine and bring to a quick boil. Put the skillet into the oven and bake for 5 to 8 minutes. Return skillet to the stove. Remove seafood from the pan and set it aside. Add parsley to the skillet, and reduce wine by ⅓. Add cream, stirring constantly until sauce reaches desired thickness. Arrange salmon on plates with shrimp and clams on top. Pour sauce over fish and decorate with crawfish. Serves 4.

THE MORRIS STREET TEA ROOM
Anderson

**THE MORRIS STREET
TEA ROOM**

When you visit The Morris Street Tea Room, be sure to watch for the ghosts carrying pink umbrellas and dancing about the grounds. Legend has it that these playful spirits are the deceased members of the eccentric Morris family, who occupied the distinguished-looking structure in the late 1800s.

The Morrises were transplanted from sophisticated Charleston society to what they considered "common" Anderson. Perhaps the dance with pink umbrellas was a fashionable number performed by Charleston high society of the day. I would have loved to have seen the ghosts, but no such colorful sight appeared. Nevertheless, my disappointment faded as soon as I entered the old mansion and found a dining room decorated in the loveliest shades of— you guessed it—pink.

Pink is not the only color you'll find inside the restored house. You're bound to come across your favorite color combination in one of the four dining rooms, each named after one of the mansion's former owners. The Caldwell Room, with its pale pink walls and rose-colored tablecloths, seemed the most romantic. I didn't mind, though, being led to the cinnamon-hued, draped table in the Johnson Room, which gets its name from the original owner, who founded Anderson's first female academy.

Heavenly smells drifted from the kitchen, where owner Angie Finazzo carefully prepares her culinary masterpieces. Some of the most requested items on the luncheon menu are the quiches. After one bite of the petite Mademoiselles Quiche, a delicious blend of cheeses, eggs, cream, shrimp and crab, I understood why the Finazzos are constantly badgered to market the item. One of the ingredients that makes this dish so special is the cream cheese used in the pastry crust.

The restaurant's dinner menu offers such enticing continental choices as Veal Medallions and Duck a l'Orange. An extensive wine list includes both imported and domestic wines, as well as unusual beers and ales.

I made a note to return on a Sunday, when an abundant buffet offers a variety of dishes. Each week, a different country's cuisine is featured along with the restaurant's regular offerings. Such a tempting array of good food will undermine the most dedicated dieter, so try to leave the calorie counter at home. However, if dieting is uppermost on your mind, then plan to choose from several salads that always appear on the menu and on the Sunday buffet.

The Morris Street Tea Room is located at 220 East Morris Street in Anderson. Lunch is served from 11:00 a.m. until 2:00 p.m., Tuesday through Saturday. Sunday buffet is served from 11:00 a.m. until 2:00 p.m. Dinner is served from 6:00 p.m. until 9:00 p.m., Monday through Saturday, but on a reservation-only basis on Monday, Tuesday and Wednesday. Reservations for the other nights are not required, but are preferred. The phone number is (803) 226–7307.

THE MORRIS STREET TEA ROOM'S
CHICKEN SOUP FLORENTINE

2 quarts chicken broth
4 ounces tiny, thin egg
  noodles, cooked

1 bunch fresh spinach
Parmesan cheese for garnish
grated carrots for garnish

Heat chicken broth until hot. Add pasta to broth just before serving. Cut raw spinach into fine strips and place in serving bowls. Pour broth mixture over spinach, and lace with Parmesan cheese. Garnish with grated carrots. Serves 6.

THE MORRIS STREET TEA ROOM'S
QUICHE ANGIE

3 ounces soft cream cheese
1 stick soft butter
1 cup flour
6 slices bacon
1½ cups heavy cream

2 eggs, plus 2 egg yolks
½ teaspoon salt
pinch of white pepper
¾ cup grated Swiss cheese
2 tablespoons cubed butter

183

Prepare quiche crust by combining cream cheese, butter and flour with an electric mixer. Remove dough from mixer bowl and knead into the shape of a ball; wrap with protective cloth and refrigerate. While pastry dough is chilling, cook and chop the bacon and set it aside. Blend cream, eggs, salt and pepper together with electric mixer until blended. Roll out or pat chilled dough into an 8-inch or 9-inch quiche pan. Add Swiss cheese and bacon pieces; pour egg mixture over all. Place butter cubes on top. Bake at 375 degrees for 30 to 45 minutes until quiche is puffed and firm and a knife inserted in the center comes out clean. Serves 4 to 6.

THE MORRIS STREET TEA ROOM'S
ITALIAN CREAM PIE

1 9-inch, deep pie shell
1 quart half and half
4 cinnamon sticks
1 cup sugar
2 teaspoons vanilla
1 5⅓-ounce can evaporated
  milk

¾ cup cornstarch
1 cup heavy cream,
  whipped
1 square unsweetened
  chocolate for garnish

Bake the pie shell and let it cool. Heat half and half with cinnamon sticks in a saucepan until hot; do not boil. Remove cinnamon sticks, and reduce heat to simmer. Add sugar and vanilla to the mixture. Blend evaporated milk and cornstarch together until smooth. Add to warm mixture and stir until thick. Pour into the pie shell and chill until set. Top with whipped cream. Shave chocolate curls and garnish as desired. Yields 1 pie.

FARMERS HALL TEA ROOM
AND RESTAURANT
Pendleton

**FARMERS HALL
TEA ROOM**

I t's easy to mistake Farmers Hall Tea Room and Restaurant for the official looking courthouse it served as in the 1820s. No other building on my historic restaurant tour looks less like an eating establishment. Situated on the village green in downtown Pendleton, the towering white structure with enormous concrete columns is the oldest farmers' hall in existence today.

It was no small feat to transform the austere concrete lower level into a warm and inviting restaurant. But owner Carolyn Fulmer, a former cooking teacher and caterer, has done just that. Cheerful yellow walls display the work of local artists. Bright green shutters are bordered by colorful crewel draperies at the windows. The sound of bustling long skirts, worn by the student hostesses, evokes a more romantic era.

The Pendleton Farmers Society purchased the stately structure more than 150 years ago, after district changes precluded the need for the courthouse. Its members still meet upstairs—no doubt after stopping below for some tasty victuals.

I arrived at Farmers Hall in time for lunch and had no trouble whatsoever making a decision. When I saw the Chicken Salad, overflowing from a white, shell-shaped dish, arrive at a table across the room, I knew I had to have the same. My choice was right; the salad turned out to taste as good as it looked. The delicious combination of chicken chunks, chopped vegetables and slices of apple, banana and kiwi was surpassed only by the melt-in-your-mouth Sour Cream Biscuits, which have helped to earn Farmers Hall a reputation for excellent food.

Because I managed to finish everything placed in front of me, I declined when dessert was offered. But it took every ounce of my resolve to keep from changing my mind when the pastry trolley came rolling by. Carrot Sponge Cake with date-nut filling, Lemon Mousse, Coconut Cream Pie and Chocolate Tortes are just a few of the famous desserts that make this charming restaurant a favorite place for afternoon tea. In keeping with the original spirit of a tea room, no alcoholic beverages are served. On Friday and Saturday evenings, special seven-course dinners are served by candlelight.

Farmers Hall Tea Room and Restaurant is located on The Square in Pendleton. Breakfast is served from 9:00 a.m. until 11:00 a.m., and lunch is from 11:30 a.m. until 2:30 p.m., Tuesday through Saturday. Dinner is served on Friday and Saturday from 6:30 p.m. until 9:30 p.m. For reservations (preferred) call (803) 646–7024.

FARMERS HALL TEA ROOM'S HAM GRATINE

Ham Preparation:

1 3- to 5-pound baked ham	**2 4-ounce cans mushrooms**
½ stick butter	**4 tablespoons flour**

Slice ham and place one layer on the bottom of 2- to 3-quart casserole dish. Melt butter in a skillet, and sauté mushrooms about 10 minutes. Add flour, and cook until blended well. Spread mushroom mixture over ham. Cover with another layer of ham slices.

Cheese Sauce:

4 tablespoons butter	**2 cups grated Cheddar**
4 tablespoons flour	**cheese**
2 cups milk	

Melt butter in a saucepan. Add flour and slowly mix in milk, cooking until thick. Add grated cheese, and cook until cheese is melted. Pour over ham, and heat through in a 325-degree oven. Serves 6 to 8.

FARMERS HALL TEA ROOM'S
SOUR CREAM BISCUITS

2 cups self-rising flour	**⅔ cup sour cream**
4 tablespoons shortening	**½ to ¾ cup milk**

Mix flour, shortening and sour cream together. Add milk until mixture is thick enough to cling to a spoon. Drop by tablespoonful onto a greased pan. Bake in 450-degree oven for 8 to 10 minutes. Serve immediately. Yields 2 dozen.

FARMERS HALL TEA ROOM'S PEACH CHEESE TART

8 ounces cream cheese	1 cup sugar
1 stick soft butter	1 9-inch pie shell
2 eggs	1 21-ounce can peach pie
2 tablespoons flour	filling

Beat together cream cheese, butter, eggs, flour and sugar until smooth. Pour into pie shell and bake at 350 degrees until top rises and cracks. Before serving, top with peach pie filling. Yields 1 pie.

FARMERS HALL TEA ROOM'S CHOCOLATE FINGERS

2 sticks margarine	2 cups sugar
½ cup cocoa	1 cup self-rising flour
4 eggs	½ cup chopped walnuts

Melt margarine in a saucepan; add cocoa and cool. In a mixing bowl, beat eggs and sugar until fluffy. Add cocoa mixture, flour and walnuts to eggs and sugar. Pour into a greased and floured 12-inch by 18-inch pan. Bake at 350 degrees for 20 to 30 minutes. After mixture has risen and fallen, remove from oven. When cool, cut into 1-inch by 3-inch bars. Yields 3 to 4 dozen, depending on size of cut.

PENDLETON HOUSE
Pendleton

PENDLETON HOUSE I have often wondered why the pub has remained a British institution, but I never expected to find the answer in a small, historic South Carolina town. Finding a bit of jolly old England waiting for me at the Pendleton House was truly a surprising experience.

Four colorful flags—the Stars and Stripes, Union Jack and the national flags of Scotland and Wales—wave from a porch that stretches across the front of the post-Victorian bungalow. As soon as you enter the front door, you'll feel as though you've been transported directly to England. Lining the pine walls of the broad entry hall are photographs of the Royal family and a collection of antique weapons. You could spend hours examining the artifacts and memorabilia, but chances are that their Churchill Pub will beckon you. Named after the famous prime minister, whose portrait hangs above the mantelpiece, this room makes it clear why pubs have retained their popularity throughout the British Isles.

If you can tear yourself away from the pub, an elegant atmosphere awaits in the Prince of Wales dining room. Tables tastefully set with Sheffield silver and Italian crystal lend a formal air to this large, open room. This is where dinner guests come to be pampered. Babs Macrae-Hall is the chef, her husband John is the host, and guests are considered the entertainment. It is not unusual to find the Macrae-Halls joining their guests for after-dinner coffee or a cordial in the inviting drawing room.

The cuisine at Pendleton House can be described best as a blend of continental and country food. Beef Wellington heads the list of favorite entrées, and Babs, who studied cordon bleu cooking in London, generously offered to share her recipe with us. A special course of European cheeses is a refreshing addition to the bill of fare. From a vast wine cellar, selections are available to please even the most particular connoisseur. Perhaps you will arrive on a night when the Rum Pecan Cake is featured for dessert. This moist and delicious treat is topped with fresh whipped cream, but I guarantee that you won't be disappointed if Strawberries Romanoff holds center stage.

This congenial restaurant is a place to spend an evening browsing unhurriedly, dining elegantly and lounging indefinitely. After one visit, Pendleton House is the place you will think of whenever you hear others speak of the wonderful country pubs of Great Britain.

Pendleton House is located at 203 East Main Street in Pendleton. There is one seating for dinner. Required reservations are accepted for hours between 7:00 p.m. and 8:30 p.m., Monday through Saturday. The telephone number is (803) 646–7795.

PENDLETON HOUSE'S BEEF WELLINGTON

2 pounds beef tenderloin
salt and pepper to taste
3 tablespoons butter
1 tablespoon cooking oil
8 ounces commercial liver
   pâté

1 sheet commercial frozen
   puff pastry
1 egg, beaten
watercress for garnish
1 tomato for garnish

Place meat on a cutting board, and remove excess fat and sinewy parts. Sprinkle with salt and pepper. Tie the meat with twine at intervals, carrying the twine around the ends and across the other sides as a package would be tied. Heat 2 tablespoons of butter and the oil in a skillet, and sauté the meat until it is browned all over, turning frequently. Put the meat in a roasting pan and dot with a tablespoon or so of cubed butter. Cook in top rack of the oven at 400 degrees for 10 minutes. Remove, let cool and remove twine.

In a small bowl, mix pâté with a fork until smooth. Using a small butter or palette knife, spread some of the pâté over the top and sides of the meat. Roll out thawed puff pastry to about ⅛-inch thick in a rectangle large enough to completely cover the meat. Place the meat with pâté side down in the center of the pastry, and spread the pâté over the remaining side of the meat. Brush one side of the pastry with beaten egg and fold the unbrushed side over the meat. Fold up the second side and press together. Trim the ends of the pastry at an angle, and save the trimmings. Brush the upper surfaces of the trimmed ends with beaten egg, and fold diagonally to seal. Raise the oven temperature to 425 degrees. Shape leftover pastry into leaves. Place them on the center of the meat and brush with egg wash. Bake in the center of the oven for forty minutes or until pastry is golden. Serve on a flat platter and garnish with watercress and sliced tomatoes. Serves 4.

PENDLETON HOUSE'S SMOKED SALMON PÂTÉ

½ pound smoked salmon
¼ cup finely chopped dill
dash hot pepper sauce
2 tablespoons aquavit
1 8-ounce package cream
   cheese

juice of ½ lemon
½ cup chopped scallions
6 slices toast
½ cup chopped capers,
   drained
½ cup chopped onions

Combine all ingredients except the toast, capers and chopped onions in a food processor or blender. Blend to a fine puree. Pour the pâté mixture into a serving dish, smoothing the top. Cover with foil or plastic wrap and chill. Slice toast into bite-sized pieces. Serve chilled pâté with toast, chopped onions and capers on the side. Yields 2 cups.

PENDLETON HOUSE'S STRAWBERRIES ROMANOFF

1 pint fresh, ripe
   strawberries
¼ cup sugar, plus 1
   tablespoon

¼ cup Grand Marnier or
   Cointreau
1 tablespoon grated orange
   peel
½ cup whipping cream

Wash, clean and dry the strawberries and place them in a bowl. Add ¼ cup sugar, Grand Marnier or Cointreau and orange peel. Fold together gently. Cover the bowl and chill in the refrigerator. Whip the cream with an electric mixer, adding the remaining tablespoon of sugar while beating. When ready to serve, top strawberries with a dollop of whipped cream. Serves 4.

CALHOUN CORNERS RESTAURANT
AND PUB
Clemson

CALHOUN CORNERS RESTAURANT

Back in the early 1800s, before Clemson was an educational center, undisputedly it was "Calhoun Country." Eight hundred and fourteen acres of rolling hills make up Fort Hill, the estate of South Carolina's most illustrious statesman, John C. Calhoun. This fiery orator, who persuaded Congress to declare war on Britain in 1812, continued to fight against tyranny until his death.

The senator's staunch defense of states rights endeared him to Carolinians, who felt the oppression of high tariffs until Calhoun worked out a compromise in 1832. So strong, in fact, was the love for this colorful senator that even today Calhoun Corners Restaurant retains his name for their establishment. Originally, the whole area was called Calhoun. But after Thomas Clemson, John Calhoun's son-in-law, donated land for an agricultural university, it became known as Clemson. Today, Calhoun's Fort Hill mansion is the focal point of Clemson University.

When Calhoun Corners Restaurant was built in 1893, it was constructed of handmade brick and was designed to be used as a social center for the community. After a few years, however, it became the home of the Fort Hill Presbyterian Church for an interim period. When the church relocated, the building was converted into a general store. Today, it is again a social center, as many consider this delightful restaurant and pub the "in" place to dine in Clemson.

When L. E. Pollard purchased the historic structure in 1974, there was no need for major structural changes. The brick walls, wooden plank floors and lofty ceiling beams probably look much the same as they did at the turn of the century. The current décor reflects a comfortable, country atmosphere. A collection of American Heritage plates, some depicting scenes of antebellum mansions, decorates the walls. Look for the plate that pictures the home of John Calhoun.

If you arrive at a time when Calhoun Corners is crowded, just wait upstairs in the bar and lounge. On Friday and Saturday nights, you will enjoy having your requests played on a piano in the intimate loft area.

The kitchen at Calhoun Corners has a reputation for producing the most wonderful prime ribs of beef. While the restaurant takes particular pride in their tender cuts of steak, seafood lovers will be happy to find fresh seafood entrées on the menu. For those who prefer fowl, take it from one who knows, the Chicken Marinara is a delicious and unusual preparation.

Lunch at Calhoun Corners mainly features sandwiches. The hottest selling item in the sandwich department is the Hot Vegetarian Sandwich, which is apt to make a vegetarian out of the most dedicated meat eater. The staff advised me that soups are also popular. I enjoyed a steaming bowl of Rosy Onion Soup, spiced with oregano to give it a special zip.

Calhoun Corners Restaurant and Pub is located at 103 Clemson Street in Clemson. Lunch is served from 11:30 a.m. until 1:45 p.m., Monday through Friday. Dinner is served from 5:00 p.m. until 10:00 p.m., Monday through Saturday. For reservations (for dinner) call (803) 654-7490.

CALHOUN CORNERS RESTAURANT'S
CHICKEN MARINARA

1 cup orange juice
¼ cup lemon juice
¼ cup maraschino cherry
   juice
1 cup soy sauce
½ cup sherry
¾ cup pineapple juice
1 cup red wine
¾ cup sugar

1½ teaspoons monosodium
   glutamate or salt
½ teaspoon garlic powder
1 3- to 4-pound chicken, cut
   up
2 slices pineapple
2 cherries
1 tablespoon brown sugar

In a large, flat, glass dish, combine all ingredients except chicken, pineapple, cherries and brown sugar. Stir mixture until well mixed. Add chicken; cover and refrigerate for 24 hours, turning chicken periodically. Remove chicken from marinade and place in a baking dish. Add pineapple, cherries and brown sugar over top. Cover with foil, and bake in a 350-degree oven for 40 to 50 minutes until chicken is done. Serves 4 to 6.

CALHOUN CORNERS RESTAURANT'S
POTATO CELERY SOUP

5 medium potatoes, peeled
  and diced
5 medium onions, diced
4 cups chicken broth
6 stalks celery, diced

1 tablespoon butter
2 cups sour cream
2 cups half and half
salt and pepper to taste

In a soup pot, cook potatoes and onions in chicken broth until barely tender. Add celery and continue to cook until completely tender. Partially mash the potatoes, and add butter. In a separate bowl, combine 2 cups of the soup mixture with the sour cream. Whip with a whisk until thoroughly blended and smooth. Pour into soup. Add half and half; stir over low heat. Do not boil after sour cream and half and half are added. Season with salt and pepper. Serves 6 to 8.

CALHOUN CORNERS RESTAURANT'S
ROSY ONION SOUP

1½ tablespoons butter
4 large onions, diced
2 cups water
1 10-ounce can chicken
  broth
1 teaspoon oregano

¼ cup sugar
1 10-ounce can diced
  tomatoes
1 cup tomato puree
dash Tabasco sauce
dash salt and pepper

Melt butter in a soup pot. Add onions and sauté until tender. Add the remaining ingredients. Simmer for 2 to 3 hours. Serves 4.

GREYLOGS
Caesar's Head

GREYLOGS

Greylogs was not originally on our list of historic restaurants. But the enthusiasm of restaurants in nearby Greenville prompted me to follow the winding road to the rustic mountain-top hideaway.

A good whiff of crisp mountain air and a glimpse of the rambling log house surrounded by towering trees were all I needed to realize my tips had paid off. The handsome multi-leveled cabin, constructed of logs from the poplar and locust trees that thrive in the area, was built in 1925 as a summer vacation home for the prominent Greer textile family. I was told that this mountain-loving family also financed the construction of the highway leading to the cabin.

Current owners Hal and Joyce Douglas discovered the log home while bringing their sons to a nearby summer camp. Unable to erase the image of the cabin from their minds, they left their Florida home and returned to Caesar's Head Mountain to purchase Greylogs in 1977.

Inside, I found a stone fireplace rising at least twenty feet to meet giant log beams. Scattered throughout the rooms is an eclectic mixture of treasures collected by the well-traveled Douglases. Somehow the 35-year-old moose head that overlooks the main dining room seems quite at home in this mountain lodge setting.

A crackling fire and bright red tablecloths provided the warmth I needed on the chilly autumn afternoon. The November weather took nothing away from the summertime feeling inside the bright, plant-filled Florida Room. This garden dining room leads to the spacious deck, where guests can dine alfresco in the spring and summer months when the mountainside is ablaze with first dogwood, then azalea and rhododendron blossoms.

Greylogs' cuisine, prepared by a marvelous Jamaican chef, is a combination of South American and French styles. You will find no printed menus. Instead, a blackboard near the entrance announces the bill of fare, which usually consists of three or four entrées, a choice of appetizers and fresh vegetables. An impressive wine cellar will please the most discriminating palate.

The congenial owners were not about to let me go without a sample of Greylogs' creamy Cheesecake with raspberry sauce and an aromatic cup of freshly ground Colombian coffee. Mrs. Douglas even managed to slip a hearty slice of Bourbon Nut Cake into my handbag for later.

Be alert for the small, unpretentious marker with the restaurant's name. It stands at ground level and seems to blend right into the landscape. If you expect a large billboard, you will most likely pass right by the entrance, as I did. Turning around is not the easiest maneuver on a mountain road, so be forewarned. But be assured, on visiting Greylogs you'll be let in on one of the best kept secrets around.

Greylogs is located off Highway 276 at Caesar's Head, and it is open from early spring until Thanksgiving. Dinner is served from 6:30 p.m. until 9:00 p.m., Tuesday through Sunday. Sunday brunch is served from 11:00 a.m. until 2:30 p.m. For reservations (required) call (803) 836–3728.

GREYLOGS' VERY VERY CARROTS

1 pound young carrots	2 tablespoons butter
3 stalks celery with leaves	¾ cup sweet vermouth
1 small onion, minced	1 cup seedless green grapes,
⅓ cup sugar	halved

Peel carrots and slice into ¼-inch pieces. Finely dice the celery stalks and leaves. Place all ingredients except grapes in a medium saucepan with the vermouth. Cover and cook over low heat until just barely tender, about 15 to 20 minutes. (Add a tablespoon of water if necessary.) Before serving, add the grape halves and heat for one minute, stirring until heated. Serves 4.

GREYLOGS' GREEN RICE

6 tablespoons butter
1 cup chopped onions
1 cup chopped celery
2 cups cooked white rice

salt and pepper to taste
dash oregano
1 cup chopped fresh parsley

Melt butter in a large sauté pan. Add onions and celery and sauté until tender. Add rice, salt, pepper and oregano; sauté, stirring constantly, until slightly browned. Combine parsley with rice mixture until well blended. Serves 4.

GREYLOGS' GASPARILLA SHRIMP

24 large shrimp
1 pound cracker crumbs
½ cup chopped fresh garlic
¾ cup chopped fresh
   parsley
⅛ teaspoon ground cloves

1 5⅓-ounce can evaporated
   milk
1 large egg
1½ cups cooking oil
4 broiled tomatoes
1 cup commercial chutney

Peel and devein the shrimp and set aside. Combine cracker crumbs, garlic, parsley and cloves in a medium-sized mixing bowl, and mix well with a fork or spoon. Combine milk and egg in a small bowl and beat together with a whisk until well blended. Heat oil in deep fat fryer. Dip shrimp, one at a time, into milk wash. Roll in crumb mixture and fry in deep fat fryer until done, approximately one minute on each side. Fry only a few shrimp at a time. Serve immediately with broiled tomatoes, chutney and Green Rice (recipe above). Serves 4.

INDEX

Hot Apples and Ice Cream, Paddock 100

Strawberries Romanoff, Pendleton House 192

Pies:

Derby Pie, Side Porch 135

"I Did It" Ice Cream Pie, Inn at Washington 172

Italian Cream Pie, Morris Street Tea Room 184

Lemon Chess Pie, 82 Queen 27

Lemon Meringue Pie, Seven Oaks 176

Mud Pie, Chart House 31

Peach Cheese Tart, Farmers Hall Tea Room 188

Peanut Butter Pie, Hartzog's Tea Room 159

Sawdust Pie, Piazza Tea Room 167

Sté. Honoree Pie, Perdita's 56

Pie Crusts

Chocolate Wafer Crust, Inn at Washington 172

Graham Cracker Crust, Turtle Deli 79

Quiche Crust, Morris Street Tea Room 183

ENTREES

Egg Dishes:

Broccoli Ham Quiche, Turtle Deli 79

Ham and Cheese Omelet, Capitol Restaurant 104

Quiche Angie, Morris Street Tea Room 183

Fowl:

Breast of Chicken à l'Orange, Paddock 99

Canette à la Lie du Vin, Philippe Million 60

Chicken Diane, Newton House 95

Chicken Kiev, Pace House 164

Chicken Marinara, Calhoun Corners 195

Chicken Oskar, Parson's Table 3

Chicken Pie, Jasmine House 84

Duckling Muscadine, Anchorage House 71

Marinated Chicken, Loading Dock 108

Poulet Sauté aux Champignons, Inn at Washington 171

Meat:

Beef Wellington, Pendleton House 191

Chili, Molly Morgan's 148

Ham Gratine, Farmers Hall Tea Room 187

Lamb Chops with Mint Sauce, Seven Oaks 175

London Broil with Mushroom Gravy, Village Inn 127

Ribs with Barbecue Sauce, Homeplace 143

Smoked Pork Loin with Glazed Apricots, Cassena Inn 19

Spartan Burger, Pace House 164

Stuffed Green Peppers, Greenhouse 116

Veal Francais, Paddock 100

Veal Medallions with Raspberry Sauce, Wine Cellar 68

Veal Princess, Up Your Alley 120

Miscellaneous:

Pasta Primavera, Pawleys Island Inn 23

Pasta with White Clam Sauce, Villa Tronco 112

Cheese Sauce, Farmers Hall Tea Room 187
Cocktail Sauce, McPherson's Dry Dock 88
Court Bouillon, Marianne 48
Lobster and Shrimp Cream Sauce, John Cross Tavern 76
Marinade for Chicken, Loading Dock 108
Mint Sauce, Seven Oaks 175
Oil and Vinegar Dressing, Oliver's Lodge 11
Orange Sauce, Paddock 99
Oyster Sauce, Cassena Inn 20
Poppy Seed Dressing, Side Porch 136
Raspberry Sauce, Wine Cellar 68
Sauce à la Bonne Femme, Marianne 48
Spaghetti Sauce, Capitol Restaurant 104
Steak Sauce, Hartzog's Tea Room 160
Vinaigrette Dressing, Newton House 96
White Clam Sauce, Villa Tronco 112

SOUPS

Broccoli Chowder, Newton House 96
Buttermilk Soup, Anchorage House 71
Chicken Soup Florentine, Morris Street Tea Room 183
Cream of Mushroom Soup, Loading Dock 107
Cream of Zucchini, Arthur's on Main 92
Garden Vegetable Soup, Turtle Deli 80
Onion Soup, 1109 South Main 179
Oyster Stew, McPherson's Dry Dock 87
Potato Celery Soup, Calhoun Corners 196
Rosy Onion Soup, Calhoun Corners 196
Seafood Gumbo, Loading Dock 108
She-Crab Soup, Rice Planters 7
Shrimp Bisque, French Quarter 40

VEGETABLES

Baked Beans, Homeplace 144
Charleston Red Rice, Middleton Place 52
Consommé Rice, Graystone Steak House 152
Deep Dish Brown Rice, Greenhouse 115
Fried Grits, Henry's 44
German Potato Salad, Side Porch 136
Ginger Carrots, Middleton Place 52
Great Potato Head, Dendy Corner 155
Green Rice, Greylogs 200
Squash Medley, Jasmine House 84
Stir-Fried Vegetables, East Bay Trading Company 35
Stuffed Potatoes, Molly Morgan's 147
Sun Rice, Chart House 32
Tangerine Yams, Cassena Inn 19
Vegetable Casserole, West Side Bowery 124
Very, Very Carrots, Greylogs 199